D1827522

STATE OF THE ART

Geoffrey Chaucer

STATE OF THE ART

GEOFFREY CHAUCER

A guide through the critical maze

Anne Rooney

THE BRISTOL PRESS

The Bristol Press is an imprint of
Bristol Classical Press, 226 North Street, Bedminster, Bristol BS3 1JD

British Library Cataloguing in Publication Data
Rooney, Anne
    Geoffrey Chaucer. – (State of the art series)
    1. Poetry in English. Chaucer, Geoffrey 1340?-1400 –
    Critical studies
    I. Title II. Series
    821'.1

    ISBN 1-85399-002-7
    ISBN 1-85399-003-5 pbk

Printed and bound in Great Britain by
Billing & Sons Ltd, Worcester

Contents

List of Abbreviations Referred to in the Text

BD	Book of the Duchess
ClT	Clerk's Tale
CT	Canterbury Tales
FranklT	Franklin's Tale
Gen Prol	General Prologue
HF	House of Fame
KnT	Knight's Tale
LGW	Legend of Good Women
MancT	Manciple's Tale
MerchT	Merchant's Tale
MilT	Miller's Tale
MLT	Man of Law's Tale
NPT	Nun's Priest's Tale
PardT	Pardoner's Tale
ParsT	Parson's Tale
PF	Parliament of Fowls
PrT	Prioress' Tale
RvT	Reeve's Tale
ShipT	Shipman's Tale
SumT	Summoner's Tale
Tr	Troilus and Criseyde
WBT	Wife of Bath's Tale

All quotations are from *The Riverside Chaucer*, edited by Larry D. Benson and others (1987).

Chapter 1

'After my makyng thow wryte more trewe': Chaucer and the Critics

Chaucer 'criticism' began during the poet's life, with the famous accolade of Froissart, 'grant translateur', and has continued ever since. The most perceptive of the early readers were not what we would now call critics, but poets in their own right, men whose careful reading of Chaucer was figured forth not in academic discussion but in new poems. To understand their reading of Chaucer now requires a double criticism: we must first understand their own poems if we are to see how they read Chaucer.

The great development in Chaucer criticism came in the 19th century, though as the collections of criticism from a broad historical span by Caroline Spurgeon (1925), Derek Brewer (1978) and John Burrow (1969) demonstrate, the discipline was already old by this time. The most important and enduring work of the Victorian critics was in establishing the texts, tracing sources for Chaucer's works and pinpointing historical events of significance to his poetry; facts which are now common property, available in every annotated edition of Chaucer's works. Our study starts with the first of the 'modern' Chaucer critics, the Edwardians. In the years since they wrote, Chaucer criticism has become a veritable wicker House of Rumour, crowded with hundreds of men and women talking at once, some no doubt speaking truth, but giving place to no single voice of 'gret auctorite'.

A Pattern of Criticism

During the 20th century, Chaucer criticism has moved away from the Victorian mode of source and historical study, through concerns with the concepts of realism and unity, taking in close reading techniques, and finally seeming to fragment with the search for a Chaucerian 'poetic' amongst rhetoric, plurality, contingency, aesthetics, medieval thought and literary tradition.

The earliest seminal work on Chaucer we shall look at is George Lyman Kittredge's *Chaucer and His Poetry* (1915), which could be considered the initiator of modern criticism. Kittredge's dramatic and 'realist' approach has now gone out of fashion, and his frequent paraphrases of Chaucer now seem irritating and patronising, but much of what he says remains good sense – so much so that many of the commonplaces of Chaucer criticism have their origin in Kittredge's work. Another critic who has suffered – or enjoyed – a similar fate is C.S. Lewis, whose *Allegory of Love* (1936) has been, if anything, over-influential with critics and students alike. Much of the best work of these earlier modern readers has become common currency now: no one feels the need to mention Lewis when talking of Criseyde's insecurity or to acknowledge that it was Kittredge who first described the marriage debate in the *Canterbury Tales* (*CT*).

If Kittredge began modern criticism of Chaucer, one of the most influential books in shaping it since then has been Charles Muscatine's *Chaucer and the French Tradition* (1957). Muscatine's study stresses the importance of Chaucer's debt to French literary forms and traditions, and directs attention back to the literariness of the works, an aspect obscured by earlier realist concerns in criticism. Muscatine detects a Gothic shape in Chaucer's narratives and an element of tension in his style. The Gothic structure has since been explored further – most notably by Robert Jordan in *Chaucer and the Shape of Creation* (1967). Since the 1960s, critics have explored Chaucer's debt to individual writers, and to various literary traditions and genres. His language has been studied to show the emergence of a specifically English poetic voice and vocabulary, to reveal his techniques as translator and adaptor, and to analyse his prosody. The exploration of the historical background has ranged from the search for pertinent events which might elucidate references, to the study of intellectual contexts such as astronomy, science, memory patterns and rhetoric. There is not world enough and time to look in detail at all of these approaches, and this book must of necessity be selective. While I aim at a representative sample , there are doubtless worthy scholars and arguments I have neglected. And – though I am not going to retract this book – I would say with Chaucer that if anything displeases the reader, attribute it to my 'unkonnynge and nat to my wyl, that wolde ful fayn have seyd bettre if I hadde had konnynge'.

Approaching Chaucer

Some of the critical methods I have just mentioned will need no introduction when they appear in the following pages. Every reader can recognise a source study, or an attempt to assign a specific historical significance to an allusion or image. Others (for example, exegetical or linguistic criticism) are less obvious, and many are found in books or articles which address more than one of Chaucer's works, and so their treatment elsewhere in this book may be fragmentary or partial. It will be worth pausing to look at a few topics and approaches in outline before embarking on the pilgrimage to Canterbury.

Some contexts: historical, intellectual and literary
Although straightforward historical criticism has long been out of fashion, there is still a place for historical knowledge in Chaucer criticism. Robert Payne (1979) argues for a type of historical awareness that does not limit the ways in which we allow ourselves to read Chaucer, but opens up new possibilities. We can divide the background which allows us to be historically aware into three categories: details of Chaucer's life; knowledge of intellectual attitudes and disciplines; and familiarity with texts and types of literature Chaucer would have known.

The first of these is the least useful. Despite the impression given by many biographical studies, we know little about the details of Chaucer's life. All the facts are collected in Crow (1966), which gives the texts of contemporary references to Chaucer with extensive explanatory notes. There are many biographical studies, all necessarily speculative. One of the more recent and comprehensive is Donald Howard (1987). In common with other biographers of Chaucer, he fills in the gaps in our knowledge with conjecture based on social history, and indulges the pleasant but deceptive tendency to believe we can recreate Chaucer's character from our experience of his poetry. (George Kane (1965) warns against the temptation to infer biographical details about Chaucer from the presentation of his dreamers.) Howard's style is naive and a touch romantic: 'Imagine [Chaucer], then, in his twenties, back from the wars, with *Le Roman de la Rose* open at his elbow, turning the French verses into English ones...'.

If we imagine Chaucer with *Le Roman de la Rose* at his elbow, we might also think of his bookshelves stocked with Boccaccio, Boethius, Ovid (or the *Ovid Moralisé*), Dante, Macrobius, Alan de Lille, Machaut, and perhaps even 'Lollius'. Since Chaucer's narratives are in a large part derivative, we can learn a great deal from what he read. Once we know which material he borrowed and from where, we can compare his words with those of his sources and assess the effects he achieves by adaptation, omission, allusion and organisation. And it would seem that Chaucer expected, or at least wanted, his readers to be aware of the intertextuality of his works. Sometimes the full force of his irony is only available to those who recognise an allusion or borrowing. Most attention has been given to his literary and intellectual debt to Boccaccio and Boethius, though many other writers have been subjected both to Chaucer's 'borrowing' and critics' scrutiny. At its best, source study hopes to show the effects Chaucer achieves and intended to achieve, how he read and understood his source material; even at its worst, it can give us valuable raw material from which to draw our own conclusions. But it is better to read the sources themselves. The most comprehensive collections are Robert Miller (1977) and Bryan and Dempster's (untranslated) sources and analogues of *CT* (1941). Also useful are Barry Windeatt's sources for the dream-poems (1982) and parallel-text edition of *Troilus* (1984), and Nick Havely's translations from Boccaccio (1980).

Chaucer's historical context does not consist only of literature. Science and pseudo-science, religion, philosophy, social and political history were all parts of Chaucer's experience which critics have found accommodated in his writings. Medieval scientific and pseudo-scientific knowledge of many types has been found relevant to a study of his poetry by Walter Clyde Curry (1926) and Mahmoud Manzalaoui (1974). Curry finds from medical theory, for example, that the Summoner's skin condition would have been seen by a medieval audience as a direct consequence of his dietary habits and womanising. In some areas, Curry's work has not been superseded, but astrology and astronomy are large topics which he could not cover fully and these have since been more comprehensively treated by Chauncey Wood (1970) and

J.D. North (1988), whose book will probably replace Wood's. Wood finds Chaucer sceptical about astrology but with some respect for astronomy. North's book is in two parts, the first tracing the development of Chaucer's cosmological knowledge and the second looking at its application, interpreting astronomical and astrological references in his poetry. The first part is densely technical, the second is a rigorous identification of dates and explication of their significance.

Another intellectual context some critics have found relevant is exegesis, a method of elucidating the Bible by reading it allegorically. The practices of biblical exegesis are brought to bear on medieval literary texts by a school of exegetical (or patristic) criticism. It is sometimes called Robertsonian criticism, after the American critic D.W. Robertson who gives a lengthy and comprehensive formulation of the patristic principle in *A Preface to Chaucer* (1962). Robertson argues that medieval poetry elicits a rational, not emotional, response from the reader, and that by interpreting a sequence of symbols and iconographic emblems in the texts we are led by reason to the lesson of charity. The whole issue is highly contentious, and many readers find the insistence on severe moral intention and the denial of realism or emotional appeal in medieval literature accords ill with their experience of the texts themselves. Several critics have pointed out that, had Chaucer himself intended all his works exclusively to direct the reader towards charity, he would hardly have felt it necessary to retract them.

Chaucer's language and prosody

Chaucer was clearly aware that language changes over the course of time. Fortunately, there are good glossaries to elucidate those of Chaucer's terms which are no longer current. The most accessible and useful on a day-to-day basis is by Norman Davis (1979). But there is more to appreciating Chaucer's use of language than knowing the common meanings of his words; studies of nuances of meaning, prosody and linguistics can all enrich our experience of the poems.

Accounts of Chaucer's language cover a wide range. The more interesting for most readers are those that relate to the literary effects Chaucer achieves. Dorothy Everett (1947) notes Chaucer's sensitivity to and talent for emulating tone of voice, vocabulary, accent and appropriate rhythms from speech and other verse forms. Paull Baum lists 'Chaucer's Puns' (1956, 1958), but does not analyse their effect. J.D. Burnley (1979) explores the 'architecture of language' – the associations, nuances and developments of meaning that give a word resonance to those familiar with its contemporary use, and Derek Brewer (1974) examines the different uses of a single word, 'sad', to show how Chaucer established 'metonymic structure', building up his own resonances for words he used repeatedly. Ralph Elliott (1974) follows a minimal introduction on pronunciation, grammar and prosody, with a discussion of the poetic effects of Chaucer's selection and use of language, examining such areas as the use of slang and colloquialisms, literary and courtly terms.

Other approaches are via a more technical, linguistic interest. J. David Burnley (1983) studies Chaucer's grammar and syntax, giving an examination of his language and vocabulary in their contemporary social and geographical context. Gregory Roscow (1981) demonstrates Chaucer's syntactical constructions with little interpretative commentary. J. Kerkhof (1966/82) provides an indispensable reference work in his study of Chaucer's language. This is systematically divided into parts of speech with extensive description and examples of Chaucer's usage. Sandred (1985) gives a more advanced and demanding study of the morphology and phonology of Chaucer's language. On pronunciation, Helge Kökeritz (1962) gives a simple guide to the rules with phonetically spelt examples to use alongside a recording.

Chaucer's prosody is an area of specialist interest, made difficult by our inadequate knowledge of pronunciation, the significance of manuscript punctuation marks, and the comparative importance of stress-based and syllable-counting verse forms. A good survey of prosodic study by Alan Gaylord (1976) reveals the major gaps in this area and makes a plea for more intelligent development, specifying several particular lines of investigation, but there have been no substantial advances since.

Early prosodists tended to impose their own standards of metre and scansion on Chaucer's verse and then emend the verse to fit; modern prosodists find a more fluid metre, generally based on iambics. Paull Baum (1961) finds a standard iambic line in the mature verse, used with considerable metrical variation, sometimes merely for convenience or from laziness (Baum appears to have little admiration for Chaucer's poetry). Ian Robinson (1971) gives a better account, finding the mature line a 'balanced pentameter' with considerable metrical variation. His book is immediately appealing because it rejects rules in favour of instinct, encouraging readers to sound final -e and place stresses so that they 'sound *right*'. He and James Southworth (1969) favour original manuscript punctuation. Although Robinson hopes to hold the interest of the general reader, he idealistically recommends reading Chaucer's poetry in manuscript, or at least in facsimile. Unlike most prosodists, Robinson demonstrates the literary effects of his findings well. Gaylord classes Stephen Knight (1973) with the prosodists, but his work, though certainly of interest to students of prosody, is as much concerned with style as technique and is in effect a 'prosodically aware' close reading.

Establishing the Corpus

It might seem odd that when so many readers can detect a distinctively Chaucerian voice there could be doubt as to which texts he actually wrote. Yet for centuries after Chaucer's death, the canon was flexible; spurious 'Canterbury Tales' went in and out of favour, and works by imitators such as Lydgate were accepted as Chaucer's own. Modern critics are confident that the main part of the corpus has now been established beyond doubt; dispute now centres on the *Romaunt of the Rose* (part A is sometimes taken to be Chaucer's, but the other fragments are rejected), the *Equatory of the Planets* and a few of the minor lyrics.

The first important work on establishing the canon and each text was Skeat's so-called Oxford edition (1899-1900); on most important issues his conclusions still stand, and his notes and glossary are still useful. F.N. Robinson made an invaluable contribution with his first and second editions of Chaucer's works, and his second edition was used as the basis of the current standard text, Benson's *Riverside Chaucer* (1987). Other editors this century have occasionally followed different manuscripts or differed in their attribution of parts of the *Romaunt* and of the *Equatory* and some lyrics. The *Riverside* follows Robinson and convention rather than current thought in printing more than the first fragment of the *Romaunt* and omitting the *Equatory*.

The most important edition of Chaucer's works will be the *Variorum* editions of each text, now in progress under the general editorship of Paul Ruggiers. There are, however, numerous editions of separate texts, from the various series of individual *Tales* to the more scholarly editions of *Troilus* (e.g. Windeatt, 1984) and the *Parliament* (Brewer, 1960). R.K. Root's edition of *Troilus* (1926) and Manly and Rickert's comparative edition of *CT* (1940) have been influential, though both have recently been criticised. A notable oddity is N.F. Blake's edition of *CT* from the unpopular Hengwrt manuscript.

The Great Translator, the Philosopher and the Astronomer

When Froissart called Chaucer 'grant translateur', he probably referred as much to the works we think of as adaptations as to those we would now class as translations, but he clearly held translation in high regard. We pay less attention to the scope of the translator's art than did Chaucer's earlier admirers. Only very recently – since 1980 – have the 'real' translations attracted any interest, and appreciation of the more closely translated parts of *Troilus* and the adaptations developed.

The best accounts of Chaucer's translation technique are by Caroline Eckhardt (1984) on the *Romaunt of the Rose*, and Tim Machan (1985) on *Boece*. Eckhardt finds Chaucer striving to maintain the feel of the French verse, but increasing the intimacy, visual imagery and narratorial presence, the last perhaps exploiting the difference between the two languages which allowed the French poet, but not Chaucer, to omit the person from the verb. Alexander Weiss (1982) studies Chaucer's use of metre and enjambment in the *Romaunt* and the *ABC*. Machan examines Chaucer's choice of words and syntactical constructions and defends Chaucer against criticisms of inaccuracy and obscurity by Bernard Jefferson (1917) and George Krapp (1915). He finds Chaucer as 'close yet as idiomatic as possible', though he considers *Boece* an experimental, rough, and unrevised copy not intended for the public in its current form. Caroline Eckhardt (1983) argues that Chaucer chose to use prose whenever he felt the clarity and educational content of his work was of paramount importance, as in the astronomical texts, and *Melibee* and the *Parson's Tale* (*ParsT*). However, Margaret Schlauch (1950) finds the greatest use of cadence in *Boece* and *Melibee* 'in harmony with their exalted tone and subject matter'. In a later article (1966) Schlauch divides Chaucer's prose into four styles, analysing each: technical, homiletic, eloquent and rhythmic.

Interest in the *Treatise on the Astrolabe* and the *Equatory of the Planets* has centred on their sources. S.W. Harvey (1935) tried to demonstrate the importance of Sacrobosco's *Of the Spheres* to the *Astrolabe*, but this is refuted by Carol Lipson (1983) and J.D. North (1988). Lipson analyses the changes Chaucer made to his source, Messahala's *Construction and Use of the Astrolabe*, and finds him increasing the clarity, accessibility and interest of the work as well as personalising it. Krapp finds it 'much more idiomatic' than *Boece*. The attribution of the *Equatory* to Chaucer is argued in Derek Price's edition (1955), and is most recently supported by J.D. North (1988). The *Riverside Chaucer* does not print it, though it is included in J.H. Fisher's edition (1982). North gives a full scientific explanation of both the *Astrolabe* and *Equatory*, placing the texts in the context of comparable astronomical treatises, and attributes the astronomical tables in the same manuscript as the *Equatory* to Chaucer.

The Elements of a Chaucerian Poetic

Studies of Chaucer's 'poetics' aim to discover his theory of literature. Literature and writing are prominent and recurrent themes in his poetry, and modern interests in intertextuality, semiotics and the reader's contribution to a text's meaning all seem to be reflected in Chaucer's own concerns, which makes this a fascinating area. The approaches to Chaucer's poetics are divergent, ranging over his attitudes to literary tradition and genre, his vocabulary and style, structure, philosophical issues, and the poet's relationship with his audience and predecessors. We have space to look at only a few of the elements here (we will encounter others later): rhetoric, literary tradition and language, structure, and the narratorial voice.

Chaucer's use of rhetoric is now acknowledged and studied, but this has not always been so. When John Manly suggested in 1926 that Chaucer knew and practised the techniques described in medieval rhetorical handbooks, the idea received a mixed reception. James Murphy wrote as late as 1964 that there is no evidence to suggest Chaucer read the rhetoricians, though the case in favour of Chaucer's rhetorical knowledge was convincingly and conclusively argued by Robert Payne in *The Key of Remembrance* (1967).

Manly denigrates rhetoric, arguing that as his career progressed, Chaucer turned away from rhetorical tropes towards realism based on experience, and came to use rhetoric only dramatically, as in the *Nun's Priest's Tale (NPT)*. Payne's view is altogether more positive. He finds Chaucer creatively alert to poetic tradition and rhetoric, and perennially interested in the relation of the poet to his material and his poetic heritage. The poet's greatest freedom is the way he can represent history and traditional stories, but Chaucer also recognised a responsibility to history and accepted that 'poetry is a process of manipulating language so that the wisdom evolved in the past will become available, applicable and operative in the present'.

Chaucer's work has also been related to more specific poetic genres and traditions, including the French dream-poems, fabliaux, epic, story-collections, the Latin and vernacular estates satires, French *complaintes* and *ballades*, Menippean satire, apotheosis motifs, and the English verse romances. Charles Muscatine (1957) identifies the contrasting demands of courtliness and realism and traces these to French courtly literature and the fabliaux. Helen Cooper (1983) analyses *CT* as a story-collection, Jill Mann (1973) compares the *General Prologue (Gen Prol)* with estates satire, James Wimsatt (1968) examines Chaucer's debt to French courtly poetry, John Steadman (1972) puts Troilus' ascent in the context of the apotheosis tradition, and F. Anne Payne (1981) shows Chaucer's relation to Menippean satire, a nihilistic genre which knocks down conventional orders and structures but offers nothing in their place. Alastair Minnis (1982) shows Chaucer depicting Classical antiquity in the light of established contemporary beliefs about the pagan world. Chaucer's debt to the English verse romances, in relation to language, motifs and sometimes narrative structures, is discussed in Patricia Kean (1972) and David Wallace (1986) amongst others. Kean finds Chaucer forging a poetic voice for English and developing elements of the native English tradition, (for example the fluid, realistic and sometimes crude everyday language of verse romances) alongside a continental high rhetorical style. Chaucer emerges as an innovator in the development of English poetry in combining high philosophical seriousness with comedy and realism. Yet that 'realism' may be, at least in part, just another literary tradition. Morton Bloomfield (1970) points out that it is often a selected 'realistic' literary style, as artificial as many others. The 'bourgeois' style identified by Muscatine is an example of this. Chaucer used many 'authenticating' devices to create an illusion of reality which does not deceive us, but also used genuine realism elsewhere. These authenticating devices include the 'real' experience of dream, the 'historian' narrator of *Troilus and Criseyde* (*Tr*) and the frame narrative of *CT*, but Chaucer is innovative in 'combining the truth claim of his major authenticating device with a circumstantial realism'.

Several recent critics have found a clue to Chaucer's poetic theory in the structures of his poems. For Joerg Fichte (1980), it is the organising act of poetry that is important. He sees Chaucer's poetry as a quest leading from 'a limited awareness of the power of poetry to the recognition that the poetic act equals the paradigmatic act of creating order in a world characterized by confusion. Only through the imposition of artistic order can the chaos lurking beneath the often smooth rhetorical surface of poetry be controlled'. This polarity – between order and chaos – is only one of the many which have been interpreted as shaping Chaucer's works. Burlin (1977) sees the contrast between authority and experience as central, though he finds Chaucer demonstrating that the antithesis is actually illusory. Traugott Lawler (1980) sees unity and diversity as the organising polarity of *CT*, and many have seen true and false felicity, or secular and religious love as the extremes explored in the *Parliament of Fowls* (*PF*) and *Tr*. Other models for structure have been the Gothic and the inorganic (Jordan, 1967). Gothic patterns do not have a central focus, but are built up from infinitely multiplying motifs. *CT* clearly lends itself easily to this type of formulation. Jordan (1967, 1987) describes Chaucer's poems as series of rhetorical or artistic blocks which make no attempt at organic unity.

Perhaps the most contentious element of Chaucer's poetic structure is his use of the narratorial voice. Kittredge recognised a narratorial figure in the dream-poems which he separated completely from the 'real' Chaucer, but it was E. Talbot Donaldson who first described 'Chaucer the Pilgrim', an intermediary narrator in *CT* (1954). Donaldson (1954) analyses the character of the Pilgrim and finds his function 'to present a vision of the social world imposed on one of the moral world'. Chaucer achieved this through layering; a surface of straightforward response to the other pilgrims is undercut by irony to elicit a different, more complex response from the reader. Many critics have welcomed this new 'character' with open arms; others have been more circumspect, and some reject him outright. It is becoming less common to accept the narrator as a constant presence in *CT*; he is more often seen now as a voice, or a shady presence that appears when necessary and then disappears without trace back into the text. For some he represents only a rhetorical device, to which critics have given embodiment. The same dispute revolves around the narrator of *Tr*, and the status of the dreamer-narrators is similarly contested, though in the case of the dream-poems the continuing physical presence and actions of the narrator figure change the terms of the argument a little: the dreamer in these poems is clearly 'there' in some sense, but how consistently? And, finally, who is he?

Chapter 2
'I kan a noble tale'

I kan right now no thrifty tale seyn
That Chaucer, thogh he kan but lewedly
On metres and on ryming craftily,
Hath seyd hem in swich Englissh as he kan
Of old tyme, as knoweth many a man;
And if he have noght seyd hem, leve brother,
In o book, he hath seyd hem in another.

(MLT, 46-52)

The Text, the Tellers and the Tales

Many readers approach the *Canterbury Tales* not in its entirety, as a story collection, but through the individual tales. Perhaps, after beginning at school with a single tale and the portrait of its teller yanked out of the *General Prologue*, the new reader is likely to find the scope of the whole work intimidating and its structure complex and puzzling. It is difficult even to assess its scope, since the text as it has reached us appears to be fragmentary: it fulfils neither the plan detailed in the *Gen Prol* to give each pilgrim four tales, nor that implied later of a single tale each, nor even the most basic topographical movement from London to Canterbury. Which of these plans, if any, Chaucer intended to fulfil it is impossible to say. *CT* has been considered to be both infinitely extendable and as complete as Chaucer ever meant it to be.

As the twenty-four tales and fragments of tales we have represent all of *CT* that we are ever likely to find, analysis of the work's structure poses some exacting problems: how can we assess the success of a work which may be less than a quarter finished or, on the other hand, may be complete? In the first part of this chapter we will encounter different ways of tackling the whole text and its unifying 'idea'. The second and third parts of the chapter return to the more familiar ground of tellers and their tales.

There is little space for detailed assessments of individual tales and their tellers, though some approaches to these will emerge from the treatment of larger topics and we will finish with a consideration of several readings of the *Clerk's Tale* (*ClT*). If a single lesson emerges from the variety of approaches we shall encounter it is that *CT* is infinitely rich; the critic is exhausted long before exhausting the poem. Finally, the completeness or integrity of the work is so uncertain, its proper order and form so precarious and elusive, that critical analysis must remain contingent, conjectural and, ideally, humble. This is a state of affairs which I feel Chaucer – with his interest in the contingency of all knowledge and the elusiveness of truth – would have liked.

The 'lytel tretys' of the 'Tales of Caunterbury'

What types of unity – or, more accurately, cohesion – can we find in such a fragmentary work as *CT*? Whatever our answer, it should take account of the possibility that tales were planned which Chaucer did not get around to writing, as well as making something meaningful of the parts of the poem that survive. Some readings of *CT* accomplish this by working from the small unit – the tale or teller, or a group of tales and their tellers – towards the larger entity. Dramatic and psychological readings focus on the characters of the tellers and the fitness of their tales and their relationships with other pilgrims, discovering a pattern which could conjecturally have been extended. Genre studies examine Chaucer's treatment of different literary forms, sometimes postulating a full exploration of narrative variety. Thematic studies trace the recurrent motifs and interests that thread through groups of tales, and attempt to assess the scope of the philosophic vision of the whole. We shall return to these types of criticism later. A more ambitious approach to *CT* is to identify the 'idea' of the text: its aim, unifying principle or controlling philosophy. Any attempt to assess the scope and final form of *CT* must begin with its structure, and the first obstacle in determining this is the order of the tales.

The order and structure of the Canterbury Tales
As the tales are not preserved in the same order in every manuscript, and no sequence apparently has Chaucer's authority, the question of the order in which the tales should be read has

been contentious. The two most usually favoured sequences are the Ellesmere order and the Chaucer Society order. The Ellesmere order is used in the *Riverside Chaucer*, and numbers the fragments I – X. The Chaucer Society order gives the fragments letters, A – I. The correspondence between the two arrangements of *CT* is:

I	II	III	IV	V	VI	VII	VIII	IX	X
A	B1	D	E	F	C	B2	G	H	I

    (I/A – *General Prologue, Knight, Miller, Reeve, Cook*
    II/B1 – *Man of Law*
    III/D – *Wife of Bath, Friar, Summoner*
    IV/E – *Clerk, Merchant*
    V/F – *Squire, Franklin*
    VI/C – *Physician, Pardoner*
    VII/B2 – *Shipman, Prioress, Thopas, Melibee, Monk, Nun's Priest*
    VIII/G – *Second Nun, Canon's Yeoman*
    IX/H – *Manciple*
    X/I – *Parson*)

A further complication is the so-called 'Bradshaw shift', which moves fragment VII to between II and III (following the order of A, B1, B2 in the Chaucer Society sequence). Robert Pratt (1951) argues for the Ellesmere order incorporating the Bradshaw shift, i.e.:

I	II	VII	III	IV	V	VI	VIII	IX	X

Early debate of this question argued for either the Ellesmere or Chaucer Society order, and for or against the Bradshaw shift. There is still life in the argument: in 1981, Larry Benson suggested the conclusive authenticity of the Ellesmere order, and in the same year N.F. Blake disputed that *any* order could be seen as having Chaucer's authority.

Arguments for and against each postulated sequence originally centred around the discrepancies of geographical location and time reference in individual fragments. Critics and editors have re-ordered the fragments to try to maintain the integrity of the actual route from London to Canterbury (sometimes including the return journey) in the occasional references to place and time of day, though more recently this type of literal approach has given way to a preference for thematic links or contrasts, and manuscript evidence.

It may not at first seem very important which order the tales come in. If one tale is displeasing, Chaucer encourages the reader to turn over the leaf and find another. But it quickly becomes clear that the tales are intended to reflect on each other, and will not yield their full meaning if read in isolation. The *Miller's Tale* (*MilT*) so obviously parodies the Knight's that it must clearly follow immediately if it is to have its full impact. The importance of deciding on the order of *CT* is evident from the effects critics claim to achieve from the sequences they suggest.

Order is inevitably linked with the evolution of *CT* as a group. Since Chaucer left the collection unfinished, who is to say he had finalised the order of the existing tales? Charles Owen (1977) begins from this premiss, suggesting that Chaucer's interests changed as the work progressed. Owen rejects the usual assumption that the plan of four tales for each pilgrim and a return journey to London was an early idea abandoned in favour of a single tale and a one-way ticket to Canterbury. Instead, he argues that the plan described in the *Gen Prol* is the revised one, and that the reference in the Parson's headlink to the completion of the game is an early and unrevised relic. Owen suggests a sequence spread over five days, going to and from Canterbury. He traces Chaucer's changing concerns, claiming that he became less interested in the religious motif of pilgrimage and more interested in the 'game' of the storytelling. The work would have finished not with the *ParsT* but with a tale which remained unwritten, and the conclusion of the contest at the Tabard Inn. The Wife of Bath's character and the tales of fragment VII would have provided a focus for the return journey.

Helen Cooper (1983) also sees a close link between the evolution of *CT* and the order of the tales, though her point is rather different. She suggests that the order was never finalised by Chaucer, but was to be based on the most fruitful juxtapositions. She postulates an experimental, partially arbitrary method of composition, and imagines Chaucer shuffling round the tales he had, to see what would result from various combinations, creating links when something meaningful emerged. She detects evidence of earlier, and of unwritten, versions in the work we have. Cooper goes on to enumerate the links, contrasts, continuities, inversions and other relationships between the tales in each fragment, and to trace themes which recur through *CT*.

Judson Allen and Theresa Moritz (1981) go to medieval commentaries, principally on Ovid's *Metamorphoses*, to find a model for the unity of *CT*. They claim that the tales fall into four groups: natural, magical, moral and spiritual. The four themes are demonstrated in the *Knight's Tale* (*KnT*), and thereafter Chaucer deals with each in turn. Within every group of tales, the main theme is transformed through its different treatments, generally being devalued. The prologues are seen as analogous to the tales and should guide our reading of them, and the tales are linked into a chain by recurring themes, motifs and references. The new sequence Allen and Moritz list to demonstrate their four groups is, in relation to the Ellesmere order:

I – natural
VIII, V, III, VI – magical
II, IV, IX & Shipman's Tale – moral
Rest of VII, X – spiritual.

They cite scanty manuscript evidence to support parts of their re-ordering. More valuable, in effect, than the central thesis are their readings of the individual tales and accounts of connections and comparisons between neighbouring tales in the fragments.

Since we cannot be sure how Chaucer intended the sequence to run, the best we can do now is to read the tales in the order printed (usually the Ellesmere), while keeping an eye open for clues that might suggest some other arrangement, particularly around the disputed area of fragments VI and VII. We should also bear in mind Donald Howard (1976), who warns that it may be misleading to find significant correspondences between tales and use them to support a chosen order: almost any order will yield some resonances, but the critic's task is the more difficult one of recognising the right order and right significance.

The idea of the Canterbury Tales

The search for a central organising principle in *CT* is more than a straightforward search for unity. The plurality of interests and voices in *CT* makes unity a dubious proposition, and indeed many of the suggestions we shall meet revolve around dualities and polarities: experience and authority, unity and diversity, seriousness and comedy, order and disorder. But unless we are to treat the work as simply a heterogeneous collection of stories, we must find a principle, or idea, which links the tales in some way. There have probably been as many organising principles postulated as there are tales; here we can only look at some of the more influential suggestions.

The earliest form of unity suggested was dramatic unity. Kittredge (1915) saw *CT* as a 'Human Comedy' in which the tales are speeches communicating the characters of the tellers. This structural model initiated the many 'dramatic' readings of tales and their tellers, a critical approach that has persisted until quite recently. We shall look at dramatic criticism more closely in the second part of this chapter, which focuses on the pilgrims themselves.

The unity bestowed on *CT* by a dramatic interpretation is an anachronistic form which Chaucer could hardly have aimed at. A more appropriate idea that first challenged the dramatic theory is in Ralph Baldwin's view (1955) that pilgrimage is not only the narrative principle but also the spiritual centre of the poem. He sees the pilgrimage to Canterbury as a metaphor for man's pilgrimage of life, beginning with the world and sensuality in *Gen Prol* and moving towards the final goal of the Holy City. The variety of experience and character shown in the tales is all finally accounted for in *ParsT* where the sins the pilgrims have exposed or confessed are castigated. The penitential voyage is completed with a penitential sermon and finally with the poet's own last act of penance in retracting his works. *ParsT* is appropriately withheld until all the pilgrims demand it, seeing it as the fit conclusion to their journey and so freely choosing the right way.

There is much in *CT* that does not fit Baldwin's structure. He concentrates on *Gen Prol* and *ParsT*, but most of the tales wander off the conjectural pilgrimage route to the Holy City and indulge in a spot of sinful wayfaring. Baldwin falls back on the idea of dramatic unity to bring the wayward tales back into the company. Paul

Ruggiers (1965) more explicitly yokes the pilgrimage metaphor with the dramatic and psychological interest of *CT*, finding that the pilgrimage sets up the frame which the drama fills in. Ruggiers also highjacks a third model for his hybrid structure, that of medieval Gothic, first suggested by Charles Muscatine (1957).

The Gothic form, championed by Muscatine and then Robert Payne (1967), represents a different type of unity. Instead of a fixed focus, it offers multiple perspectives and open patterns. Both Muscatine and Payne quote from Arnold Hauser's description of Gothic as a 'panoramic survey, not a one-sided, unified interpretation dominated by a single point of view'. The applicability of this to *CT* is clear. Muscatine rejects the dramatic element, since this would reduce the possibilities open to Chaucer. The relation of tale to teller in a Gothic structure of unity is 'not idiomatic, but...tonal and attitudinal'.

Gothic form allows a multitude of perspectives and threads in a pattern, but although the edges may not be distinct, the whole is integrated. Jordan's model for *CT* (1967) stresses the elements of Gothic which tend away from integration (1967). He finds the basis for a unified view of *CT* 'not in the idea of "fusion" but in that of "accommodation"'. The emphasis is on juxtaposition, the 'accumulation of individually complete elements' that stresses the disjunction of units rather than their relation. If Muscatine's model is the intricacies of Gothic architecture and interlace, Jordan's Gothic is a snipped-up interlace – a leaf here, a stray tendril there – making up an 'inorganic' construct. This last model, the snipped-up Gothic or inorganic, has now become the dominant one in studies of *CT*. A glance at a few more recent studies will show the directions in which it is developing.

The title I have borrowed for this section, *The Idea of the Canterbury Tales*, belongs to a book by Donald Howard (1976) which looks for a pattern for the organisation of *CT* in such models as the Gothic flower design, the interlace pattern, the double columns or facing pages of a book, and the penitential 'pilgrimage' labyrinth designs found in some Gothic cathedrals. The key element in these structures is 'juncture': the conjunction of two units which are set side by side but not joined. The interlace pattern of *CT* is developed as themes recur in different tales, are revisited and finally undermined or degenerate towards the end of the work. The tales have different types of closure, directing us back to the frame or on to the next tale, or to realms outside the poem, as do elements in an interlace design. Thus fragment VII emulates the structure of the whole poem, looking back and revisiting themes, finally parodying and undermining the effect of what has gone before. This prepares the ground for *ParsT* (a new book, a 'juncture'), which shows that 'the tales were lies' and truth is in the reason and authority of religion. Howard concludes that Chaucer is attempting something new and difficult in suggesting that 'a book about the world could really be for our "doctrine" because it could present us with an idea of the world against which to measure our idea of ourselves, and so teach us who we are'.

Howard's models are often characterised by duality. Other critics, too, have found antithetical positions organising *CT*'s multifarious elements. Sometimes such readings seem to acknowledge our desire for unity which conflicts with the work's resistance to a unifying interpretation. This is true of Joerg Fichte's reading (1980), which sees an opposition of order and disorder in the poem, where poetry can gain the upper hand and impose order on chaotic existence. He sees *CT* presenting various types of disorder, including the contentiousness of the pilgrims, intellectual myopia, natural disorder (such as a young bride married to an old man) and cosmic disorder (the unfair determinism of the *Man of Law's Tale* (*MLT*)). The ordering process is shown as 'an artistically contrived juxtapositional pattern of heterogeneous material'. The artifice is clearly visible: 'The juxtapositional, additive principle Chaucer employs...make[s] the disjointedness of the parts more visible; the parts are then forcibly integrated into the artistic structure in order to emphasize the powerful forces of disorder always threatening to destroy this design'. *KnT* shows order imposed on disorder as Chaucer attempts to 'create an *ars poetica* which operates on the assumption that the ever-threatening specter of disorder can be neutralized within a tight-knit poetic structure'. The 'sermons' at the ends of *ClT*, *KnT* and *Tr* 'are substituted for thematic resolutions' for the same reason: 'Chaucer thus forces an ending on recalcitrant and thematically dissonant material in order to hide the fact that his poetry is basically anti-teleological...non-medieval'.

Traugott Lawler (1980) finds a different, though related, polarity organising *CT*, one that again reflects the work's resistance to a single pattern: unity and diversity. This he relates to experience and authority. Authority is the result of collective or generalised experience, and although experience often endorses authority, there is also frequently a disparity between the two or between different authorities. So *KnT* polarises Egeus, the voice of authority, and the experience of Palamon and Arcite. Theseus is in the middle, learning from experience and so becoming an authority. Lawler finds *CT*'s concern with marriage relevant to his theme, since marriage attempts to make a unity from two people. The whole work is concerned, too, with the medieval professions, and here Lawler notes its affinities with fabliaux. The professional group is an 'authenticating company' which unites many, though the interaction of the individuals which represent the professions is marked by rivalry and trickery. So humankind is one species, but divided into two sexes, further divided into warring professional groups, and then into contentious individuals. The conflicts are finally resolved, though. *ParsT* fulfils expectations of closure encouraged by the pattern of diminishment in the structure, 'make[s] the final movement from many to one' (the one being Christ), and also moves decisively from experience to authority.

Alfred David (1976) also finds Chaucer's 'effort to reconcile the "auctorite" of his age with the experience of his inner vision...precisely what makes his poetry great'. In *CT* he sees Chaucer moving away from the lessons of tradition and antiquity, but with the role of the poet remaining a dominant concern. He sees an interplay between ordered seriousness and chaotic realism which allows the expression of – or exorcises – different aspects of Chaucer's vision. Thus the *Merchant's Tale* (*MerchT*) 'shows the dark side of Chaucer's genius' which is once given free rein so that it might then be banished from the 'holiday' of *CT*. Although Chaucer's concept of the poet's role emerges in fragments from the voices and perspectives of the tales, he becomes increasingly disillusioned and sceptical about the validity of poetry and so is led to retract his work.

Although readings which follow Muscatine's Gothic model make a virtue of the multifariousness that seems to threaten cohesion in *CT*, most tend, sometimes despite themselves, to drift towards resolution. An exception is Larry Sklute (1984), who makes the poem's variety its central point. For Sklute, the narrator's uncertainty shows the impossibility of ascertaining truth from the different views, and 'possibility is the central concern of the entire work and inconclusiveness is the means through which the form expresses it'. The narrator's intention is 'journalistic': he aims to tell everything without editing or judging, and there is no authoritative judgment offered in the text.

A different type of unresolved plurality is found by those who locate *CT*'s organising structure in its literary genre or ancestry. Setting the work in a literary context can help us to define the nature of *CT* and give some kind of (occasionally illusory) grasp of its elusive form. We shall look at some of these models next.

Old books and new tales

The 'olde bokes' Chaucer digested and re-formed to make *CT* are many and various. To see precisely how he used them in the case of individual tales, we need to look at the sources and analogues, helpfully collected together by W.F. Bryan and Germaine Dempster (1941), and more recently by Robert P. Miller (1977). (Lynn King Morris provides a comprehensive bibliography of source study, 1985.) There have also been several studies of Chaucer's use of the work of individual writers. There is detailed textual comparison of the tales with their sources in Boccaccio by Boitani (1977), Salter (1983) and Wallace (1985). Hoffman (1966) explicates allusions to and borrowings from Ovid, and John Fyler (1979) compares Chaucer's narrative techniques with those of Ovid. Chaucer's adoption of rhetorical theory and images from Geoffrey of Vinsauf and the other rhetoricians is analysed by Robert Payne (1967) and Robert Jordan (1987), and F. Anne Payne (1981) has assessed the influence of Boethius as a Menippean satirist. Just as influential as sources are literary traditions. The variety of narrative modes Chaucer uses in *CT* shows an experimental interest in appropriating and moulding literary forms, and is testament to an acute critical capacity to understand and manipulate the relationship between genre and matter. In *CT*, as everywhere else, Chaucer appears intensely aware of the heritage of literary tradition and what it offers him.

The most obviously analogous form is the story collection. Helen Cooper (1983) examines *CT* in the light of this genre, finding Chaucer's collection unique in mixing genres and being cast as a competition. Cooper finds the main emphasis on the diversity of literary form within the potential realm of 'story'. She sees *CT* as an encyclopaedic work which aims to present the best of every type of tale in an inclusive 'exploration of the limits of genre'. The attempt ends 'finally in the rejection of poetry and fiction – in the rejection of creative literature'. This rejection follows the questioning of the 'activity of story-telling' in the *Manciple's Tale* (*MancT*) when the Parson 'destroys the whole principle on which the *Canterbury Tales* is based'. The work is unfinishable, and Chaucer did not intend to write any more of it.

Another obvious model is pilgrimage narrative, mentioned earlier with reference to Baldwin's thesis. Howard, in his two studies of *CT* (1976, 1980), examines but ultimately rejects this as a controlling pattern; he sees the poem setting up and then confounding expectations as the inter-relations between the pilgrims disrupt the anticipated form of pilgrimage narrative and produce a new one, of disordered experience 'as it is held in being through memory'. Details of the pilgrims' inner life emerge – the psychological and moral background to a pilgrimage – in preference to the geographical and superficial details of travel narrative. There is a 'lapse into a mentalistic realm' which is not actual or literal and where the time scale becomes an artificial 'day' of pilgrimage, the pilgrims passing around the edges of towns, on the margins of civilisation. Edmund Reiss (1967) takes up Baldwin's idea of the allegorical pilgrimage, and relates *CT* to other poetic/allegoric pilgrimages. He finds that Chaucer's pilgrims embody the sins which the pilgrimage should purge and are themselves the 'counterparts of the various illustrative figures' in other allegorical pilgrimage narratives. The audience are the real pilgrims, since they can travel through and learn from the work. *ParsT* is a return to the world, and hence to the pilgrimage of Christian life. Christian Zacher (1976) also relates *CT* to other pilgrimage literature, finding a conflict between curiosity and pilgrimage. The Canterbury pilgrims do not have the right attitude for a real pilgrimage, the fellowship being characterised by mirthful disorder rather than solemn order. The narrative is not intended to be allegorical, but is rather 'an institution and custom with particular social relevance to the tales'.

As well as *CT*'s relation to obviously connected genres, comparison with styles and traditions of representation can also be illuminating. Muscatine (1957) discusses Chaucer's use of the two French styles, the bourgeois (or realistic) and the courtly, finding the use of different styles contributing to the meaning of the tales. For example, the 'naturalistic' style of the fabliaux is appropriate to their dependence on the natural world, and in each case furthers the plot: the regional dialect of the students in the *Reeve's Tale* (*RvT*) is important in that it establishes the low social status of the tricksters and so compounds the miller's humiliation.

Different comparisons can give different results when elements of Chaucer's narrative method are related to traditions and sources. Alastair Minnis (1982, 1986) analyses Chaucer's depiction of pagan antiquity, finding in *KnT* and the *Franklin's Tale* (*FranklT*) respectively a sensitive portrait of virtuous pagans drawn according to medieval beliefs about the pagan world and showing they can be as noble as any Christian. In *KnT* Theseus' near-Boethian philosophising surpasses the limitations of the capricious and spiteful pagan gods to reach towards an understanding of divine love. Thus, though the gods are condemned, the characters are not: it is only historical accident which distinguishes them from Christians. Minnis sees a contrast between the unjust pagan gods and the serene Christian truths Theseus approaches, but Elizabeth Salter (1983), who compares *KnT* with Boccaccio's *Teseida*, finds it 'an uneven work of "sad lucidity"' which expresses 'not the great orthodoxies of medieval faith, but the stubborn truths of human experience'. John Fyler, comparing Chaucer's technique with Ovid's, agrees that Theseus tries to impose order on disordered matter, but finds the Knight following the same process, carefully organising his tale to form symmetrical patterns from chaotic events.

Other traditions are less immediately relevant. Satire has offered a different type of approach to *CT*. Jill Mann (1973) has discussed *Gen Prol* in relation to medieval estates satire, and F. Anne Payne (1981) finds *NPT* and *KnT* both employing features of Menippean satire. Payne's reading (1963) of *KnT* finds many conflicts which are neither explored nor resolved. She sees the Knight discarding much of his material, concentrating his efforts on the more hopeful (or at least, less dismal) elements. *KnT* presents a collection of fragments in which Theseus tries unsuccessfully to make order of chaos and make sense of man's predicament. The poem, characteristic of the type of Menippean satire, destroys faith in the order displayed, but offers no answers and no structure to replace that lost. Mann's book concentrates on the portraits of the pilgrims in *Gen Prol* and so returns us from a wide panorama of the entirety of *CT* to the more familiar ground of individual tellers and tales. Though this may seem against the grain, we shall endeavour to prise teller and tale apart, and turn first to the pilgrims.

The 'joly body': Pilgrims and Personalities

Many of us first encounter *CT* by studying a single tale and its teller, probably examining the character of the pilgrim and its relation to his/her tale. We ask questions like: is the tale suitable to the teller? Does the choice of tale and its delivery tell us more about the character of the pilgrim? When the characters and tales are put together and seen to interact, a 'roadside drama' emerges, and this type of dramatic approach to *CT* is often appealing because it brings into play habits of reading which are familiar from our experience of novels and drama. Yet it is only one of many ways of studying the portraits of the pilgrims and their relation to their tales. Other techniques are often more appropriate, and can offer different kinds of insight, especially when we look at the pilgrims all together. There are different types of historical readings, patristic interpretations (see p. 5 above), attempts to set the pilgrims in traditions of literary and iconographic repre-sentation, and rhetorical studies which return us from the personalities to the text.

Historical realism and literary tradition

In many ways Chaucer's pilgrims seem immediately vivid and realistic, a slice of 14th-century life miraculously captured. Indeed, so lifelike have they seemed, that John Manly devoted a book to revealing the real-life figures behind the fiction. In *Some New Light on Chaucer* (1926) he cites historical figures on whom he believes Chaucer modelled the pilgrims. Now universally reviled as literary criticism, this study still gives some interesting background information: it appears, for instance, that there really was a Harry Bailey who owned an inn called the Tabard in Southwark. But on the whole, it seems unlikely that Chaucer simply transposed his fellows into fiction, and the value of the information is doubtful: would knowing the 'real' identity of a pilgrim help us to read their tale?

Another type of historical background research has been employed by Walter Clyde Curry (1926). His study of Chaucer in the context of medieval sciences draws evidence from contemporary medicine, physiognomy and astrology to show how aspects of the physical description of the pilgrims, or references to their horoscopes (e.g. the Wife's blaming her lechery on the astrological aspect of her birth), reflect aspects of their moral characters. Larry Sklute (1984) makes use of some of the same type of material, but finds that repeated use gives characteristics additional connotations, and the traditional details along with their symbolic associations may also have 'historical' applicability to the individual pilgrim. For example, the Wife of Bath's deafness *may* be symbolic of sinfulness, but it also results from a blow delivered by her last husband. This combination makes the portraits dynamic; interpretation is open-ended, with no possibility of or need for a conclusion. Muriel Bowden (1949), gathers historical information of a more general kind, though frequently following Manly. After filling in the background to the Canterbury pilgrimage and the cult of St. Thomas, she uses historical events to explain the pilgrim portraits. She also relates Chaucer's descriptions to traditions of literary representation, initiating a method of assessing the pilgrims which remains current. Her account of the Monk, for example, collects contemporary evidence of monks hunting, posing on horseback in extravagant clothes and enjoying sumptuous meals to demonstrate that Chaucer's Monk incorporates both the historical figure of the worldly monk and the literary satire that immortalised the figure.

Although the interest in historical data represented by critics like Manly, Curry and Bowden has waned, a new type of historical study, aimed not at realist interpretation but at clarifying the nature of the fiction, has emerged. A controversial book by Terry Jones (1980) aims to show how the Knight is in reality far from a noble courtly figure, but instead a disreputable mercenary whose 'mortal batailles' were massacres in which mercenaries helped (or hindered) Christian or pagan armies equally. The consequences for *KnT* are important: 'by putting a chivalric romance into the mouth of a new-style mercenary captain, Chaucer has created a cold, dark world of fear, oppression and death' and shows how chivalry and knighthood 'had become the tools of tyranny and destruction'. Jones finds the tale showing 'obsessive materialist concerns', a travesty of justice ruled over by an Italian tyrant whose 'first mover' speech presents not Boethian philosophy but 'the long-winded, sententious waffle of a conceited autocrat'. Although some of Jones' evidence is less substantial than he might like, the book is rigorously argued and his view has not been given the consideration it deserves. There has been a tendency to dismiss it out of hand, whether because it accords so ill with how most people like to read *KnT* or because medievalists resent an outsider trespassing on their territory is hard to say. However, most readers still conclude, if uneasily, that Jones is wrong.

Bowden's book, which combined elements of historical evidence with an awareness of the traditional literary presentation of the figures, has now been superseded by a more thorough analysis of the literary ancestry of the pilgrims by Jill Mann (1973). She argues that *Gen Prol* was modelled on 'estates satire', a type of literature which satirises the different social 'estates' (professions, status or social positions) through an enumeration of the faults typical of each. Chaucer borrowed many of the conventional characteristics of the estates for his portraits in *Gen Prol*, and his concentration on professional occupation mirrored the focus of estates satire. Chaucer did not use explicit moral criticism as the estates satires tended to, but more subtly suggested such conventional faults as the gluttony and lechery of monks through his use of language. Indeed, we are invited to condemn and condone at the same time. Chaucer used the pilgrims' own voices for their portraits, attaining apparent effects of individualisation and realism despite taking details from traditional estates satire types.

The fruit and the chaff: allegory and exegesis

A different approach which also makes use of established motifs and types is patristic criticism. This seeks to find in medieval literature a sequence of symbols with codified, ascertainable meanings that direct the reader towards the Christian doctrine of charity. For *CT*, this means that the details of the pilgrims' descriptions are iconographic, and reveal each one's moral state. D.W. Robertson (1962) demonstrates how dramatic interaction and psychological interest are excluded, as the 'figures are separated or isolated from one another much as they are in Gothic art'. In a later essay (1980) the pilgrims are seen as 'collections of attributes exemplifying either the ideals or weaknesses of the groups to which they belong'. Robertson (1962) presents the pilgrims as types – the Wife of Bath is 'a literary personification of rampant "femininity" or carnality' – and their own explanations or understanding of their tales manifest their qualities, so that the Wife's tale is 'vigorously carnal and literal' in keeping with her (im)moral nature, though their tales often reveal more about themselves than they intend or realise.

The fullest exegetical treatment of *CT* is by Bernard Huppé (1964). He sees all the pilgrims moving towards Judgement, and the 'interplay between the literal and spiritual meanings [of pilgrimage] provides the thematic touchstone by which the gallery of pilgrims may be judged'. Huppé detects two types of drama in *CT*. The first is the interaction of the pilgrims, related by the naive narrator. The second is the 'drama of their inner lives' communicated to us by Chaucer in, for example, their choice of tales and response to their own and others' narratives. Huppé detects a pattern in which the less 'realistic' tales – such as *KnT* – contain 'real' philosophical truth, whereas the more realistic – such as *MilT* and Wife of Bath's (*WBT*) – display only a superficial world view and   partial understanding of the other tales they answer or complement. Sometimes the audience or reader responds in a superficial way which is corrected by the text. For example, we despise Griselda's obsequious patience, but the true message of the tale is that she is, nevertheless, the model we should strive to emulate, and we must replace our superficial view of her conduct (grovelling obedience before a tyrannous husband) with an understanding of her proper patience before God. Huppé gives a reading of all the tales he finds interesting (or susceptible to his type of exegesis), and although these cannot be summarised here, two other examples of exegetical readings will serve to demonstrate the method. The first endorses feelings most readers share about the Pardoner; the second produces an unlikely interpretation of *NPT*.

In an influential article, R.P. Miller (1955) shows that the *Pardoner's Tale* (*PardT*) has a 'consistent philosophical pattern artistically presented through the manipulation of Scriptural images' which demonstrates that the Pardoner is a Scriptural eunuch – spiritually sterile and unproductive of good works. The Pardoner is depicted as the *vetus homo* (old man) contrasted with the Christ-like *novus homo* (new man). The *vetus homo* deliberately cuts himself off from God's grace, thus the Pardoner is aware of the gift of the Holy Ghost but rejects it. This is the only unremissible sin, and he is, as Kittredge said, a lost soul. Whether or not we accept the details of Miller's argument, few would contest the evil of the Pardoner. Mortimer Donovan (1953) achieves a more unusual result with his reading of *NPT*. He seeks 'a doctrinal idea' suitable to a priest, and since he has already decided what he will find before he opens the book, we may feel that his explanation is foisted on a poor, defenceless poem. By reference to patristic and biblical authority, Donovan discovers that 'Chauntecleer stands for any holy man alert to temptation and Daun Russell for the tempter, the "povre widwe"...suggests herself as the Church'. The tale shows the 'holy man alert to temptation' susceptible to sensuality (Pertelote's advice) and so vulnerable to the fiend. Though he falls, he prays and is inspired; he does not remain fallen.

In his refutation of exegetical criticism, E. Talbot Donaldson (1960) takes issue with Donovan's article. He argues that it distorts *NPT* to make it fit the theory (in, for example, accepting the Nun's Priest's account that the tale blames Pertelote). The tale is also over-long for the point Donovan maintains it is making: if 'it is the main point and the little anecdote on which the exegesis depends is only one tiny grain of wheat in an intolerable deal of chaff...then [Chaucer] is guilty of most horrid misproportioning'. The real point, he says, is the rhetoric which Donovan would reject. Rhetoric is shown to be an 'inadequate defence that mankind erects against an inscrutable reality'; it enables a man (or a chicken) 'at best to regard himself as a being of heroic proportions...and at worst to maintain the last sad vestiges of his dignity'. For Donaldson, then, 'the fruit of the *Nun's Priest's Tale* is its chaff'.

The roadside drama

Reading the tales psychologically and dramatically has been immensely popular. Such readings assert that each tale is chosen and told in such a way as to demonstrate the nature of its teller's character, a character further exposed through interaction with other pilgrims in the frame narrative. Where the relation of tale to teller is not clear, it is taken that Chaucer would probably have returned to the tale to shape it more precisely to its teller. Dramatic readings in particular attempt to demonstrate the realism of the characters of the tellers and tend to subordinate individual tales to the pilgrims and the frame: 'the Pilgrims do not exist for the sake of the stories, but vice versa' (Kittredge, 1915). The most systematic dramatic treatment of *CT* is by R.M. Lumiansky (1955). Lumiansky does not consider the tales more important than the tellers (or vice versa), but thinks that part of the function of each is to support the other. He describes three stages of dramatic evolution to account for the different levels of compatibility of pilgrim and tale: firstly, the tales and tellers are well-suited to each other; secondly, some tales are motivated by the pilgrims' own personal relationships, such as professional rivalry; thirdly, Chaucer achieves a complete dramatic revelation through the triple combination of *Gen Prol*, tale prologue and tale. The least sophisticated teller/tale combinations operate on only the first level, with the tale explicating a single dominant trait of the character (e.g. the Second Nun and the Squire). Slightly more complex are those which use only this level but demonstrate a double trait in the character (such as the Knight and the Prioress). Where rivalry or antagonism between two characters colours the tales, the second level is also involved (as in the cases of the Cook and the Manciple). The most sophisticated combinations achieve all these levels (Wife of Bath, Pardoner, Merchant and Canon's Yeoman). Lumiansky gives an account of the dramatic personality of each pilgrim, building up his picture from *Gen Prol*, link passages and tales. Sometimes the tale is so well-suited to the teller that we exercise psychoanalytical skills to discover a 'full-scale character revelation that goes beyond the intention of the story-teller'. In other cases the relation of tale to teller is less well developed, but Lumiansky manages to find evidence of the teller's character in every tale. The link passages and the Host are important principles in maintaining the dramatic unity. The Host's character, particularly his ineptitude as a self-styled literary critic, is lambasted in the tales told by Chaucer as pilgrim in his own narrative, and is elsewhere developed through his responses to the tales and their tellers.

There have been numerous studies of the psychology of individual tellers and the suitability of their tales, and yet more that take the psychological or dramatic context as the basis for explorations of a different kind. Earl Birney (1960), for example, analyses Chaucer's irony; but it is the correspondence between the character of the Manciple and the attempt of his tale to be 'gentil' which underlies his exploration of the language of *MancT*. The approach is indeed persuasive, and is often the first to appeal to the reader more familiar with 19th-century than medieval literature. Some of the conclusions of dramatic readings have been rewarding, though their significance can still be disputed: it is clear that *WBT*, the story of a woman gaining mastery over her husband, reflects interests projected in the Wife's prologue, and that the story the Pardoner tells would have a very different effect if it were not used subversively for immoral ends. We might, though, prefer to see this disparity of material and purpose as an intellectual or rhetorical exercise rather than a working out of the Pardoner's psychology. The 'roadside drama' approach to *CT* has come in for severe criticism recently. The art of *CT*, it is argued, does not reside in 'photographic' reproduction of actual people travelling an actual journey, but in what Chaucer made of the fictional situation of people on a pilgrimage. This may combine some realism, including a dramatic element, with artifice, since Chaucer did not aim for simple verisimilitude. Donald Howard (1976) coined the useful term 'unimpersonated artistry' to denote the artifice which we accept not as part of a mimetic depiction but as part of the literary art: 'In its simplest form [unimpersonated artistry] is the contingency that a tale not memorized but told impromptu is in verse...In its more subtle uses it allows a gross or "low" character to use language, rhetoric, or wit above his capabilities'.

'Roadside drama' criticism will not quite lie down and admit to defeat. There are now some more complex versions from which the cruder realist element has been expunged. Robert Burlin (1977) sees the tales as 'psychological fictions' which reveal the pyschology of their tellers.   This is not to create a dramatic situation, but rather to allow Chaucer to explore the effect of character on tale-telling. The focus of critical interest has shifted from the characters themselves to what is perceived as Chaucer's real concern – the process of fiction-making. Another recent revision of dramatic criticism by H.M. Leicester (1980) takes issue with the 'unimpersonated artistry' brigade, finding the multi-plication of narrators (poet; Chaucer-pilgrim; other pilgrims) an unnecessary complication. His post-structuralist reading inverts the usual procedure of dramatic criticism, working backwards from the voice of the tale to determine the nature of the teller. Leicester sees *CT* as 'a collection of individually voiced texts', and begins with the very textuality that has previously been cited as undermining the coherent drama of *CT*. Finding that 'there is nobody there…there is only the text' he works from the language of the text to create characters: '[the tales] concentrate not on the way pre-existing people create language but on the way language creates people…it is the tale that specifies the portrait, not the other way around'. There remains something of a problem with the Chaucer-pilgrim narrator. Unoriginally, Leicester identifies ironies and complexities which prevent us deciding exactly Chaucer's position or the status of this voice. However, this mystery is at least realistic: in life, as in literature, we cannot see and assess an individual's stance with certainty and clarity.

The return of rhetoric
Leicester's conclusion that 'there is nobody there' returns us from personalities to the voice of the text. Jordan (1987) distinguishes between a persona and voice in this way: 'while a persona is a fixed entity that generates *a priori* interpretative expectations, voice is a flexible instrument…that forms and transforms itself in the ongoing movement of a text'. Identifying a Chaucerian voice rather than a Chaucer-pilgrim, Jordan argues that *Gen Prol* and the tales present changing voices distinguished by differing rhetorical techniques. The body of the tales reverts to the Chaucerian voice, and it is not possible to distinguish, say, Chauntecleer's voice from the Nun's Priest's voice. The tales manifest Chaucer's interest in the gap between 'knowing and showing', a problem of perfect articulation. This interest surfaces sometimes, as in *PardT* where the demonstration of vice expressing virtue reveals Chaucer's 'awareness of the ambiguous mediating function of language'. Jordan identifies a binary structure in the relationship of discourse to story, or subject to object: 'in counterpoising story and discourse, fiction and fiction making, Chaucer deliberately plays on the inherent discourse ambiguity of narrative (in contrast to the de-emphasis of this aspect of textuality in a nonrhetorical poetics)'. David Lawton (1985) also finds many voices in the tales, but identifies these as tones and 'voices of performance', engaging the audience and moulding response. In place of characterised narrators he finds 'ostensible tellers' sometimes apparent at the start and finish of a tale, but the features which dramatic readings assign to personalities he interprets as simply stylistic or rhetorical

qualities. He divides the Chaucer-pilgrim into two, after the manner of *Le Roman de la Rose*, with a present voice and a recalled past self who saw, heard and experienced the pilgrimage.

If we read the tales in terms of rhetorical voices, we are likely to find in their tone an indication of their intention rather than a key to character. Lee Patterson (1983) finds the voice of *WBT* using rhetorical techniques common to other figures playing comparable roles, such as the Vieille in *Le Roman de la Rose*. The traditional garrulousness of women is, he finds, always associated with sexuality. Such figures mix frustration and enticement, attraction and repulsion, carnality and morality in their rhetoric, mimicking the ambiguous ways in which women are perceived, and eliciting a similarly ambiguous response. However, the Wife's rhetoric employs masculine devices (e.g. her appropriation of authorities) to further her own, feminine, ends (defeating authority). With this debunking of dramatic characters as critical foci we are returned to the tales themselves, narratives told by voices not to reveal personality but to achieve a purpose, create an effect and make a poem.

'Tales of best sentence and moost solaas'

The striking diversity of poetic form and genre in *CT* has an entropic energy of its own: the different forms pull in different directions, so that we may find it hard (or irrelevant) to locate any kind of unity in the work. Another consequence is that it is easy to read individual tales as integral units, demanding little reference to their context in the larger work. Detailed examination of one or two tales has often produced the most inspiring and inspired of all contributions to Chaucer criticism. It can reveal a self-contained poetic achievement, or contribute to a reading of the whole poem. We have space to look at very few of the huge number of such studies, but shall examine three ways of considering the style and texture of single tales or small groups of tales: setting them in relation to their genre (taking the fabliaux as an example); tracing their relation to other tales in *CT*; examining different types of detailed analysis of an individual tale (using *CIT* as an example).

Generic variety and exploration

Earlier in this chapter we examined some suggestions about the governing idea of *CT*. One possibility is that generic variety is the central issue. If Chaucer was trying to establish the boundaries of the definition of 'story', he also managed to stretch the categories and surpass our expectations of the genres he employed in his quest. Critics who find the diversity of genres a central focus of *CT* point to fragment VII as an exploration of poetic variety. Helen Cooper (1983) sees the tales of fragment VII foregrounding the relationship of matter to meaning as well as dealing with other literary questions such as the 'status of language'. There is greater diversity of genre in this fragment than in any of the others, and within it *NPT* acts like a miniature *CT*, incorporating different types of narrative within the one tale. Alan Gaylord (1967) also finds the fragment unified by its interest in the art of story-telling and dubs it the 'Literature Group'.

Chaucer's concern with the potential of different narrative modes is clearly an issue. Robert Payne (1963) sees Chaucer blurring the distinctions between the major genres (romance, fabliau, saint's legend) with, for example, more rhetoric in the fabliaux than was usual for the genre. He finds Chaucer 'experiment[ing] with the relationship of stylistic elaboration to the basic narrative structure underlying it'. The results of his experiment are, most successfully, 'an almost diagrammatic demonstration of theme without any stylistic emotionalization' in the *PardT*. This can be contrasted with an 'exaggeration of emotion to near-lyric proportion' in the *Prioress' Tale* (*PrT*), which he finds 'the summation of an effort...to write a purely affective narrative in which irony, characterization, and complexity of action all give way to a very rigidly controlled stylistic artifice'. Robert Jordan (1974) also sees Chaucer's narratives breaking the usual bounds of genre. Writing on the romances, he finds the diversity of their subject matter and form precludes any coherent grouping, and their additive, 'inorganic' structure further makes the term 'romance' of limited use. He ends by denying that there is really a romance group at all.

The tales which have attracted most attention recently as a group are the fabliaux, though this has not always been the case. Earlier critics, and indeed editors, often took Chaucer's advice in the prologue to *MilT* to 'Turne over the leef and chese another tale'. Though the plot structures, motifs and bawdy are clearly borrowed from the French fabliaux tradition, Chaucer makes much more of his comic tales than this alone would suggest, often developing them in directions which take them away from fabliaux tradition, as Payne's observation on their rhetorical content demonstrates. Derek Pearsall (1986) goes as far as to deny that some of those accepted as fabliaux should really be so classified at all; he finds the *Shipman's Tale* (*ShipT*), which Ian Robinson (1972) considers 'the purest fabliau of all' to be instead a delicate comedy of manners. Explorations of how the comic tales work often depend on close reading to determine the tenor of their jokes and ironies. The puns, fundamental to Chaucer's comedy, have been listed and explained (so inevitably losing their comedy) by Paull Baum (1956, 1958). Patricia Kean (1972) has shown how the fabliaux depend on timing and the narrative flow because comedy emerges from the logic of the narrative. Other interesting studies look at the imagery, language and irony of the fabliaux. Janette Richardson (1970) explores the use of imagery in Chaucer's faliaux, setting it in the medieval context of the writings of the rhetoricians. She finds that the rhetorical texts rarely look beyond the methods of textual adornment as anything other than surface ornamentation, not seeing them as crucial or contributory to the meaning of a poem or part of the aesthetic whole. Chaucer, however, transcends the rhetorical forms, choosing 'formal figurative images which have ironic relevance beyond their immediate appropriateness'. Richardson examines examples in each of the fabliau tales, and concludes that Chaucer most commonly uses imagery in this way firstly to foreshadow coming events, secondly to endorse the effects created through plot and characterisation, and thirdly to set up moral standards against which the inadequacies of the immoral characters become obvious. For example, *MilT* is full of animal imagery. Some of this is conventional, but together the images accentuate and contribute to the 'frank animality of the tale'. Individual images often have additional, local, importance. Absolon's eyes are said to be as grey as a goose (the comparison is conventionally with glass), which perhaps prefigures his encounter with the fart, since the bestiaries taught that the goose is the animal most sensitive to the smell of man. The comparison of Alison to a weasel may be more than superficially relevant, too: the bestiaries say that the

weasel sneaks around the house, lying in a different lair each night.
Earl Birney (1960) looks at the ironies in the structure of *MilT*,
finding the oppositions in the portrayal of Absolon and Nicholas,
and in Absolon's affectations and his fate, to be the source of much
of the poem's comedy. He detects a similar kind of structural irony
which makes the *Summoner's Tale* (*SumT*) effective (1960a).
Just as important in establishing the relation of the tales to their
genre is the use of elements which are not usually found in fabliaux.
E. Talbot Donaldson (1950) discusses the use and devaluation of
courtly terms in *MilT*, noting how Nicholas is saddled with the
epithet 'hende', a word invariably used to describe the hero of a
verse romance. The unsuitability of these heroic associations, yet
the word's concordance with the image of courtly lover that
Nicholas is trying to project, generates irony in the tale. Another
critic who has written on the appropriation of courtly style in *MilT*,
optimistically by Absolon and satirically by the Miller, is Ian
Robinson (1972). He locates the power of the comedy in the
destructive contrast of Absolon's high-flown courtly pleas and the
responses of Alison and her husband, giving us pleasure in
'bawdiness adulterated...with poetry'.

The tale in the Tales
As well as relating the tales as groups or individually to their genres,
we can compare one tale with another. This reveals repeated
motifs, narrative patterns and themes which help to link the tales
together and amplify their meanings. The links include the parodic
relationship between *KnT*, *MilT* and *RvT*, and Chaucer's
exploration of themes – marriage, justice and others – which make
one tale reflect on and influence our reading of another. Although
these underlying or explicit themes or questions help to hold the
tales together, they also emphasise the centrifugal variety of
opinion. As we saw earlier, Helen Cooper (1983) and Donald
Howard (1976) discern in *CT* a form of Gothic interlace structure.
In the interlace design, the parts are linked by intricate connections, and also juxtaposed, where there is no join, at junctures.
The intricate connections Cooper finds in *CT* are strands of
imagery and themes that bind tales (not necessarily adjoining
tales) together. Cooper identifies and traces themes (such as the
working of providence, or the nature of true and false felicity),
recurrent motifs (such as the girl with two lovers, brotherhood and

fellowship), and correlations between plot and imagery which work out the same ingredients in different ways concordant with different genres (as in *KnT, MilT, FranklT* and the *Merchant's Tale (MerchT)*). Kean (1972) also traces the themes of free will, Fortune, marriage, and nobility and virtue. This quality of a web of connecting themes, images and motifs has been noted by many critics, several of whom have concentrated on the exploration of just one – most notably the so-called Marriage Debate.

The earliest treatment of the marriage debate is Kittredge's essay 'Chaucer's Discussion of Marriage' (1912). Kittredge sees the Wife of Bath initiating the discussion, and the tales of the Merchant, Squire, Clerk and Franklin responding. The first four offer differing imperfect visions of marriage, and the Franklin resolves the debate with an 'ideal' version. The perfection of the Franklin's solution has been disputed since Kittredge wrote, and many now find in it yet another inadequate and partial view. Some have treated the marriage debate dramatically, relating the 'answer' each pilgrim gives to his or her character. The patristic critics find a rather different message in the marriage debate. Huppé, for example, identifies the message that men and women should not appropriate marriage to their own ends, whether to serve desire or produce an heir, but that marriage should be part of the service of God. Some feminist critics like Arlyn Diamond (1977) find Chaucer limited by his 'fundamental conservatism', treating the women with sympathy but being 'unwilling to abandon the values and hierarchies he inherits, unable to reconcile them with what he has observed of human emotion and social realities'.

Another type of link between tales can be forged by language. We have seen how elements of Chaucer's language can help to relate his poetry to the context of its genres. Chaucer sometimes used words with particularly clear associations and resonances, either pre-established in literary tradition or built up through his own metonymic structures, which carry verbal associations through from one tale to another. Words used repeatedly by Chaucer build up their own resonances. Several critics have studied this aspect of language in *CT*. Derek Brewer (1974a) has analysed Chaucer's handling of the word 'sad', concentrating on *ClT*. He finds it more often meaning 'serious cheerfulness' than with its modern sense, but more important he shows that tension between meanings and associations or connotations derived from previous contexts colour its signification when it is encountered again. Tatlock's concordance to Chaucer's works (1927) makes this type of analysis available to any reader with the patience and inclination. Anyone who wants to explore further the meanings and resonances of Chaucer's vocabulary in the larger context of contemporary English can consult the Middle English dictionary for extensive examples of usage.

The tale 'allone, withouten any compaignye'
We have already encountered several of the methods that can be applied to reading an individual tale. The psychological, rhetorical and patristic are all clear-cut possibilities; source study, and tracing the influence of literary traditions or earlier authors known to Chaucer can also be useful. Other methods employ close reading techniques and studies of form or structure. Before we explore some of these, though, we should glance at a couple of approaches that rely on historical knowledge to relate a tale to a specific historical event, one that perhaps Chaucer was unable to discuss openly. Leslie Hotson (1924) finds in *NPT* reference to a scandal concerning one Nicholas Colfox, whose name is apparently hidden in the poem. Paul Olson (1986) reads all the tales with regard to the comments he thinks they make on social events of the day; he reveals references to – even advice on – social unrest, war with France and the Peasants' Revolt, and finds correspondences between events in *CT* and events in contemporary England. Thus *KnT* mirrors the conflict between England and France in its Athens-Thebes conflict, and domestic unrest in the antagonism of Arcite and Palamon. *KnT* is therefore 'a serious critique on English policy to create peace within and abroad'.

We have seen how the patristic critics use established iconographic symbolism to explicate the tales. A more recent, influential type of iconographic reading is suggested by V.A. Kolve (1984). Kolve also seeks pre-established symbolic meanings and allusions for images in the tales, seeing visual images and iconography as central to Chaucer's narrative art. He relates this to medieval aesthetic traditions of visualising the subject matter of poetry (very literally in the case of allegorical personifications), and to the function of visualisation in memory. He finds a few central images in each tale, images which invite us to construct vivid mental pictures and which belong to an existing iconographic tradition. Their symbolic meaning does not replace their literal significance: 'the iconographical image...is characteristically assimilated to the verisimilar and mimetic texture of the whole; it is discovered *within* the images one forms in attending to the narrative action itself'. Kolve examines the first five tales (fragments I and II), describing the provenance and resonance of their central narrative images. For example, the main narrative images of *KnT* are the garden and prison in juxtaposition, and the amphitheatre. The garden and prison in *KnT* are important literally as locations, but have additional meanings. Love is both a garden and a prison, but the prison grows to include all life becoming in Theseus' words 'this foule prisoun of this lyf'. The amphitheatre, built on the site of Palamon and Arcite's duel, is an attempt to impose order, but despite his intentions a larger disorder overtakes Theseus' plan. These two images, of order imposed on but overtaken by disorder, and of the prison (garden) of life, embody the central ideas of *KnT*.

These examples of historical and iconographic significance are only possible for the reader who has a certain amount of background knowledge relating to the poem. Other types of analysis focus on the text itself, and represent the type of response any alert, uninitiated reader could have. The various types of close reading are difficult to classify, depending as they do to a large extent on the personal response of each reader. To give an idea of the range of such readings, we shall take a single example, *ClT*, and examine a few of the critical readings it has received.

The characters and plot of *ClT* were for many years dismissed as unsavoury and monstrous, the structure seen as fractured by the changes in the characters, and the cruelty too unbearable for the poem to support. Kittredge (1915) placed it as part of the marriage debate, seeing it as a riposte to the Wife's promotion of masculine submission to feminine mastery. But *ClT*'s first champion was James Sledd (1953). He argued that the behaviour of the characters did just about accord with how the tale portrayed them before the deterioration of the marriage, so that it is not radically split in two by a change in behaviour. Further, we are shielded from extremes of pain and horror by the melioration of cruelty through the narrator's transmission and by his giving us confidence that there will be a happy outcome. Even so, Sledd finds the poem characterised by 'dulness and sentimentality'. The next important interpretation was Elizabeth Salter's close reading (1962). She identifies the source of the reader's unease as the two different perspectives C/T presents; one 'absolute and symbolic', the other 'relative and realistic'. The first is articulated in the Clerk's statement that the tale is not to be taken as an example for wives but shows us how we should be obedient to God; this demands acceptance of the suffering in the tale. The second is the sense of outrage that we feel (and which the narrator expresses and encourages) in the treatment of Griselda, and our subsequent reluctance to accept her actions and suffering. Salter finds the tension in this dual perspective symptomatic of Chaucer's own difficulty with C/T and shows that he had not properly worked out what he could do with such unpleasant material.

Salter's view is reductive: it suggests that Chaucer wrote the whole tale unaware of, or unable to do anything about, his own conflicting feelings. A.C. Spearing (1972) takes up the same point about the poem's two perspectives, but finds these to be deliberate, intended by Chaucer to 'articulate a view of human life of which a distinctive feature is precisely that it feels the pull of more than a single set of moral standards'. He finds the voice resistant to the horror of the tale being established in the rhetorical additions to Petrarch's source-narrative; these additions communicate the Clerk's responses to and interpretation of the tale he is retelling. Burlin (1977) adds a third perspective, but also finds the effect derives from a deliberate juxtaposition of conflicting views. Classing it as a 'philosophical fiction', he sees it pointing to the disparity between the 'authority' of God's love and justice, and the human experience of pain and suffering to no obvious end. Although the problem we perceive here is a failing of perception, it remains one that 'theology neglects...at its peril'. Critics vary in the extent to which they make the tension between the allegorical and realistic perspectives central. Charles Muscatine (1957) identifies the style of the tale as 'conventional': non-realistic and formal. He finds style and narrative 'pared...almost to nakedness' and that its sparsity and simplicity directs us to the symbolic, so that 'the moral is generated by the style itself' and 'the whole ordonnance of the poem invites, constrains a symbolic reading'. Olson (1986) finds the symbolic aspect most important, but acknowledges our unease, adding that if we think God, like Walter, to be a tyrant it is on account of a failure in our perception.

Two other critics approach the issue through close analysis of the language. Ian Robinson (1972) sees Chaucer walking a tightrope between the symbolic and real. Griselda's language defines a close affinity with the Christian soul or presents her as 'the church in her union with Christ'. But the connection of the characters to their larger symbolic roles is restricted to the working out of a single theme, patience. They are also realistic, so rooting *CIT*'s religious element in the real world. Close examination of the language can also extend our understanding of the realistic roles of the characters. We have already looked briefly at Derek Brewer's study of the resonances of the word 'sad' in the poem. A similar study by Colin Wilcockson (1980) examines the use of 'thou' and 'ye', showing how careful choice of the pronoun communicates important information about the shifting relationship between the characters. Particularly important is the ambiguity involved in 'thou': it can be either affectionate or alienating, as Walter may be using it intimately or to emphasise the low social status of his wife.

Finally, Judith Ferster (1985) puts *CIT* in the context of more recent critical thought. She looks at three areas of the poem: the self, politics and literary meaning. She finds the mediating function of interpretation important, displaying the modern awareness that a work of literature is a compound of the words in the text and the reader's response. Griselda negates her self in her marriage to Walter, and he seeks her identity, unaware of the effect he has in changing it. She sets up the conditions for her own torments by always going beyond his demands, and re-voicing them to him in a form that further diminishes her own identity. In the political realm, too, people are manipulated by giving them descriptions of themselves, and Walter both alters and is altered by the populace. The same process operates in our understanding of the text, which is affected by what we bring to it. This point is brought home forcefully by the diversity of meanings we have seen critics discover in *CT*: 'Chaucer reminds us that when we interpret his poems, we should be mindful of our own influence on their meaning. That is, paradoxically, the only way we have a chance to see in them more than ourselves'.

Drawing the Threads Together

The diversity of critical response to *CT* both reflects and probably contributes to our experience of the poem's own plurality. It is not a coincidence that many writers have sought in the poem some attempt at reconciling unity and diversity, for this is an act we often feel compelled to perform ourselves in ordering our response to it. The recent tendency to see accommodation rather than any hierarchical ordering or other formal patterning as the principle on which the poem is organised is more challenging to our natural urge to pin down the poem, but I think it is the right approach. Any neat compartmentalising of *CT* necessarily neglects or subordinates some parts, and generally without good aesthetic grounds. *CT* certainly deals with such issues as authority and experience, the relation of tale-teller to tale, and the struggle to impose order on chaos in both life and art. But to find any one of these the single organising principle is to read (or appreciate) only part of the poem. If I had to choose an organising principle for *CT*, it would be the activity of story-telling. Chaucer's interest in the many aspects of tale-telling, from setting the boundaries of what comprises a story (from sermon to bawdy joke), through the relation of fiction to reality, the consequences of the teller's personality and moral purpose for the tale he or she tells, the relation of the new tale to its antecedents and literary tradition, to the manipulation of response through the finest details of language. *CT* is Chaucer's great exploration of what it means to be a writer, what tale-telling involves, and what it should or could achieve. This is certainly an accommodating principle rather than an organising one, and one, too, which allows us to be accommodating in our reading of the poem's critics. Within this great enterprise are the tales themselves, which can be taken out of context as magnificent examples of story-telling in their own right. We can then exercise our critical faculties in explicating the single tale and its parts, being drawn in to the work as through a series of Chinese boxes. But even when we are examining the use of a single word, we are uncovering the story-teller's art and are brought back to Chaucer's larger purpose. The poem does not close off perspectives – this is why so many varieties of response have seemed appropriate – and it would be unwise for us to close off perspectives as we read it, and so unnecessarily limit our experience of what *CT* has to offer.

Chapter 3
The 'sorwful tale' of Troilus and Criseyde

Troilus and Criseyde is regarded by many as Chaucer's masterpiece, even surpassing *CT*. But agreeing on a poem's greatness is very different from agreeing on the nature of that greatness; critical opinion of *Tr* seems irreconcilably divided. Does the poem celebrate love, or condemn secular, sexual passion? Should we approve of some, or all, or none of the characters? Is the central philosophy propounded in *Tr* one of fatalistic determinism or personal autonomy? Does the poem have a Christian message, and if so is it austere and recriminatory or hopeful and merciful? Does the poem give answers or merely pose questions? There can be few major works in which the author so successfully conceals his hand that readers cannot agree on such a fundamental point as whether the poem is hopeful or desperate in its assessment of the human condition.

Disagreement about the poem is brought into sharp focus by interpretation of its ending. The brevity and conventional sentiment of the epilogue renouncing secular love seem ill-matched with the extended and sympathetic treatment of the love-affair which has come before. It seems, in the words of J.S.P. Tatlock (1966), that Chaucer 'tells the whole story in one mood and ends in another'. The dilemma is immediately apparent: if Chaucer is serious in renouncing all that has gone before, why did he treat it at such length and so sympathetically? If the renunciation is *not* serious, how are we to read the ending? There are, broadly, four distinct critical responses: (1) The whole poem is, according to Lewis (1936), 'a great poem in praise of love' and the ending is misguided. At all times there have been critics who, like Curry (1926), have dismissed it as 'not a part of the whole...one need not...consider it at all in an interpretation of the drama'. (2) The poem condemns love; close reading reveals ironies and subversions throughout *Tr* which undermine the value of the love-affair. (3) The poem and its ending must be read together in some way as a synthesis (to show a development from secular to divine love, for example). (4) The disjunction is deliberate and meaningful; it is currently popular to try to accommodate both our natural interest in the characters and a more abstract moral or philosophical interpretation of erotic passion. Recent critics have attempted to reconcile the elements of *Tr* harmoniously, or to find meaning in the tensions.

Critical interest concentrates around *Tr*'s ending not because it is the most important part of the poem but because its apparent incongruity is the greatest test of a critic's reading. Most questions raised by the poem are related in some way to the duality of the epilogue. The treatment of sources and the narratorial voice relate to Chaucer's perception of his role as poet, but it may be his difficulties with the material that prompt the final *volte face*. We may read the poem dramatically – as an exploration of the psychology of the characters – or philosophically, with the characters performing symbolic roles in the presentation of a moral lesson, or both. But Troilus' uncharacteristic laughter waits at the end to confound our theories. The depiction of ancient Troy, and the handling of pagan religion and philosophy return us equivocally to the destination of Troilus' soul. The ending is to many readers the most difficult or enigmatic part, and any complete reading of the poem must eventually take issue with it.

To reduce for a moment the vast range of criticism on *Tr* to a simplified pattern: the 20th century has seen a shift – from a blindness to the more crucial dilemmas *Tr* embodies, through attempts at resolution and reconciliation, to an acceptance of tension and contingency as creative and meaningful. Many lines of inquiry do not fit this pattern, of course. Source study is a major example, though even here the variety of source materials can direct us back to Chaucer's problem with reconciling their conflicting demands. Since duality is such a major feature of *Tr* we shall follow Chaucer's lead and juxtapose opposites. The most far-reaching question for any text is 'what is it about?', so this chapter begins with some clearly polarised views of the moral and philosophical tone of *Tr*, and then moves on to those which attempt either to harmonise or to suspend the duality discovered. This duality also appears in the contrasting medieval and pagan elements of the story, which we shall look at next, and which will introduce the critical response to Chaucer's use of literary tradition and his specific sources for *Tr*. We shall then explore critical approaches to the issue of characterisation, whether as realistic or symbolic. The 'fourth man', the narrator, we shall consider last, returning to some of the discussions on closure and on the poet's relation to his text.

In Celebration of Love or Condemnation of Lust?

From the beginning of this century to C.S. Lewis' handling of *Tr* in his *Allegory of Love* (1936), critics found in the poem an outright celebration of love, clothed as was only natural for Chaucer's culture, in the garb of courtly convention. They read in *Tr* a display of the beauty of love, and its fragility in the face of adverse circumstance; Troilus ennobled by his love, and his service to Criseyde unquestionably right and proper.

Kittredge (1915) identifies the characteristic modes and mores of courtly love (Chaucer is assumed to have followed the only model for the portrayal of love which he knew), but beneath these finds truths about love which are perennially valid. W.G. Dodd (1913) makes more of the same stance, and excuses Troilus' ineffectual behaviour on account of his acting wholly within the expectations of the courtly love tradition. Twenty years later, C.S. Lewis (1936) finds Chaucer recasting Boccaccio's story in accordance with the tradition of courtly love. He sees the work as 'the consummation...of [Chaucer's] labours as a poet of courtly love'. The poem emerges as predominantly hopeful, a celebration of love as *fin amour*, with no inkling of unease at either the moral tone of the epilogue (which is not really confronted) or the betrayal of the great love affair.

This version of joyous celebration now seems a naive and wishful reading of a poem which ends with betrayal, death and explicit rejection of the value of erotic love. In direct contrast – but still taking account of only one side of the duality – patristic criticism sees the poem as a condemnation of indulgent and sinful cupidinous passion. D.W. Robertson (1952) argues that *Tr* follows the pattern of Boethian tragedy and the archetypal tragedy of Adam: we are shown man subjecting himself to his baser instincts, loving a created being above the Creator. Troilus' cupidinous idolatory is a result of his willingness to fall into sin: he makes himself vulnerable by looking at women in the temple; he is proud and slothful. He thus loses his freewill as a result of his own action, though he is further encouraged in his subjection by Pandarus. Attracted by Criseyde's physical beauty, Troilus does not see that she is vain and self-seeking. Chaucer wants us, as he says at the end of the poem, to give our love to Christ, the true good.

Robertson neglects much of the poem in his analysis: he does not mention the narrator, or Boccaccio, and dismisses all references to virtue as ironic. Chauncey Wood's more rigorous treatment (1984) produces an equally moral reading. He acknowledges the interest created in individual character, which Robertson largely denies, and enlists Boccaccio, Boethius, Dante and Le Roman de la Rose to support his thesis that the characters are morally misguided and ultimately corrupt and that Troilus' love is of the wrong sort. Wood charts Criseyde's desertion of moral discretion as she is undermined by Pandarus and Troilus, and argues that the whole love-affair is presented as a foolish and dangerous indulgence.

Where the critics who celebrate courtly love ignore the message of the epilogue, or acknowledge no difficulty in accommodating it in their reading, the moralist viewpoint concentrates exclusively on the tone of the ending and 'reads backwards' into the poem to find that view supported throughout. Both approaches have been criticised as narrow and selective, and few recent readers have found the poem as unambiguous as either would maintain, usually seeing the poem supporting and condemning secular love at different points. I have highlighted here the extreme positions on the 'philosophy' of Tr because the multiple ambiguities of the poem can all be related to this aspect, and seem to concentrate in such questions as whether the poem is optimistic or pessimistic, tragic or comic, religious or secular. In fact, the duality of the poem is manifest in many different ways, and over-simplifying labels of this type are unhelpful. Recent criticism has moved away from black-and-white judgments, and generally acknowledges the presence of conflicting elements in the poem. This gives the reader the freedom to decide whether to to harmonise the disparate parts or to choose between them, or resolve them in other ways.

Harmonised Contraries and Fruitful Ambiguities

Between the polarised readings of the poem outlined above lies a whole spectrum of more accommodating views. Many find the poem too complex and original to be fully explained in terms of any single model or tradition. Once critics begin to admit to the contradictions in the text – even in the reductive terms of Tatlock's view (1966) that the epilogue represents an unaccountable *volte face* – the door is open for more searching criticism. If we are not to find the epilogue inadequate, or inappropriate, we must arrive at a way in which its severity illuminates the preceding poem. We might see a development – such as human love leading to divine love – or we might seek to form a synthesis of the elements, or find meaning in the tension between them. Such readings tend to concentrate on aspects of *Tr*'s use of irony and ambiguity. What follows is an outline of some of the more important and interesting attempts to harmonise the elements of the poem or to find meaning in their conflict.

Ida Gordon's influential work (1970) on the ambiguities of the poem argues that while we sympathise with and feel for the characters, the irony in the poem directs us towards the moral message of the epilogue. We respond emotionally to the characters but rationally to their behaviour as the ironic presentation allows us to divide our fellow-feeling with them from our judgment of their actions. Chaucer directs our intellectual response through the use of irony. For example, Troilus misappropriates fragments of Boethian arguments (as when he sees his love for Criseyde as the love which binds Creation together) and in the gap between his presentation of the argument and our supposed complete knowledge of it, his limitations are demonstrated and the Boethian point is endorsed. The naivety and ambiguity of the narrator's presentation allow us alternative approaches to the same issue, event or character. But Gordon's argument falters when she claims that the narrator's defence of Criseyde represents Chaucer's own voice since 'there is no need for irony at this stage'. Again she has him speak 'as poet, not as narrator' in the 'Go, litel book...' apostrophe. Ultimately, 'the poet is encouraging these young people...not to despise the happiness that sexual love can offer, but to be sure that the good their love is seeking is the real good'. Troilus is finally responsible for his own fall; his error is that he thinks he has found divine love, and Chaucer urges us not to make the same mistake.

In the view of Donald Rowe (1976), the whole poem is composed of opposites – philosophical, stylistic and in characters – which coexist in creative harmony following the model of the universe proposed in Troilus' speech on the binding power of love. The union of Troilus and Criseyde endorses Macrobius' view that contraries are capable of union because of fundamental similarities underlying their differences. Their love harmonises contraries in a lesser image of God's harmonising in the universe, and restores Troilus to something resembling the pre-Lapsarian state. Because man is a microcosm, we see in Troilus an image of 'the union of the Word with matter to create the universe'. The whole poem shows how men are led to contemplation of God through contemplation of the world (see also Rowe (1988) on the *Legend of Good Women* (*LGW*)). Interpreting Criseyde as a symbol of the mutable world, and Troilus as the soul, Rowe argues that the only way fallen man can approach contemplation of God is through the 'mirror' of Creation. When Troilus rejects earthly love from the eighth sphere his vision is incomplete – he fails to recognise the value of the love that has elevated him.

Alan T. Gaylord (1979) finds the problems of the poem resolved in its ending rather than held in harmony throughout. For him the 'contraries are not so much tensely opposed as manifestly placed in order' as we recognise that Troilus' tragedy is his refusal to use his freewill to make a choice, and his subsequent lapse into despair. The ending places everything in its proper form, locking the pagans into their setting and returning Chaucer to the land of living poets and philosophers with Gower and Strode. Charles Owen (1957) approaches the ironies and ambiguities from a new angle when he analyses the revisions Chaucer made to the poem during the process of its composition. He finds Chaucer deliberately developing passages which oppose each other in content – for example, praising profane or religious love in turn, or establishing a dialectic on freewill and fate – in a symmetrical and balanced manner. He argues that this shows Chaucer endorsing different values which are *both* valid, though irreconcilable; the betrayals the poem records validate the religious vision, but do not invalidate human love. The opposites help to elucidate each other and render their contraries meaningful: 'the two ideals are held in a sort of tension by the poem, and only by the aid of both can we see either the full meaning of love or the full meaning of betrayal, meanings which it is the aim of the poem to define'. (This reading depends on the tradition of Chaucer's revisions first proposed by R.K. Root (1916), who identified three separate stages to the production of the poem preserved in the manuscript versions. This has since been refuted by Barry Windeatt (1979), who says that there is no evidence of a consistent process of revision.) Peter Elbow (1975) develops a similar idea, rejecting the need to harmonise the contraries, and preferring to see the oppositions as supporting each other. Chaucer simultaneously asserts conflicting ideas in *Tr*, but one idea is not denied by another; both gain support from the intelligent presentation of the opposite. He urges us not to choose between the conflicting views presented, or to try to forge a synthesis from them, but to hold both (or all) possibilities in mind at the same time, to maintain them in fluid and provocative coexistence. By contrast, David Lawton (1983) sees the reader's role as more active, finding in the multiple tones of the poem a challenge to the reader or audience to forge their own opinions using their own moral values.

All these readings see the ironies, ambiguities and tensions of the poem deliberately used by Chaucer, for one purpose or another, but Elizabeth Salter (1966) finds in them evidence of Chaucer's own problems and uncertainties with the work. She considers the ending is at variance with the depiction of love in Book III because Chaucer's purpose was 'not entirely clear to him even when the poem was well under way', and that he grew progressively dissatisfied with Boccaccio's treatment of the tale. He expanded his own poem's perspectives in spite of his source and the inevitable ending, though in Book V imaginative freedom is closed off again as the (now unsuitable) ending is imposed. Alfred David (1976), too, concludes that Chaucer could not resolve the incompatibility of his rational knowledge as a 'medieval moralist' of what 'ideally should be' and what his feelings as poet told him is true. He was 'intellectually committed to his Boethian and Christian moral, [but] emotionally committed to the Christian reality he has created'. The problem thus stands in the text, unsolved and unsolvable.

Medieval and Classical Elements

It has been common to relate some of the ambiguity of *Tr* to the coexistence of pagan and medieval strands. Amongst other effects, this coexistence involves a simultaneous exclusion of Christianity from the surface of the narrative and the assumption of Christian values in the audience and narrator. Chaucer's development of these strands has been closely related to studies of the sources for the poem and the traditions in which he was operating. These variously contribute 'medievalising' or 'Classicising' details.

The earliest important work relating the poem to its sources is C.S. Lewis' essay (1932) on Chaucer's use of *Il Filostrato*. He stresses the 'medievalisation' of Boccaccio's essentially Renaissance story, arguing that Chaucer adapts this tale to demonstrate the operation of courtly love. There are many pertinent and salient points in Lewis' essay, and he demonstrates admirably the general nature of some of the changes Chaucer made. However, he is not always able to explain convincingly the poetic effect of the alterations, identifying some changes simply as 'medievalisation' for its own sake. Further, some passages from *Il Filostrato* he considers Chaucer to have extended simply for the sake of it: 'Chaucer found his original too short and proceeded in many places to amplify it'. Lewis does not try to integrate the passages he sees as doctrinal and philosophical into the rest of the poem, but claims that a medieval audience would have found such extraneous matter interesting in its own right, and would have been grateful for the bonus of a little didacticism, without regard to the poetic unity of the work. The same point is made by Derek Brewer (1974b): he argues that apparently inappropriate passages of philosophising in *Tr* and elsewhere should be read 'vertically', not as part of the sequential or realistic depiction of the action but revealing something of the text's relation to its audience. (This relates to a model of vertical and horizontal structure formulated by Robert Jordan (1967), which we shall look at later.)

Charles Muscatine (1957) also pursues the similarity between *Tr* and French courtly tradition, examining it in the light of his contrast of bourgeois and courtly (see p. 10 above). He finds Troilus too perfect as a courtly lover. Pandarus provides a 'view of courtly love under the aspect of realism', and the two interact to produce irony and commentary on courtly love. A slightly more involved situation is proposed by Barry Windeatt (1979) who finds not merely Chaucer but Pandarus deliberately shaping Troilus and Criseyde's experience to follow the patterns of literary models for love affairs. The poem uses contrived repetitions of points in the experience of love to this effect, as when Criseyde sees Troilus ride past her window twice, once by chance and once because Pandarus has engineered it. David Wallace (1985,1986) finds a further source of 'medievalising' influence in the English verse romance tradition. The colloquialisms and tags, formulae and clichés of the romance tradition were skilfully incorporated among the Classical, Italianate and courtly elements of Tr as Chaucer forged a new poetic vocabulary, identity and credibility for English. Patricia Kean (1972) demonstrates Chaucer's creation of an English vernacular poetic language more fully.

Whereas Lewis and Muscatine pursued Chaucer's 'medievalisation' of the pagan tale, analysing his addition of French courtly detail, others have argued for a 'Classicising' or 'paganising' of Boccaccio's narrative. Winthrop Wetherbee (1984) gives a comprehensive study of both Classical and courtly influences on Tr, and finds that the Classical allusions undermine the concern with love and courtesy developed from the romance tradition, putting them into the perspective of history and heroism. Alastair Minnis (1982) concentrates on the pseudo-Classical, showing Chaucer working from a thorough medieval conception of the theological and philosophical beliefs of pagans to recreate a pagan world of convincing authenticity for his audience. Minnis' pagans are not without their flashes of insight, but they have obviously not read Boethius and are realistically limited by their lack of Christian philosophy or hope; they manage as well as historical accident allows. Troilus is as good as a pagan can be: his love is not rejected as sinful, but rather shown to be incomplete; his fatalism does not elicit criticism, though clearly the medieval reader could not share it. The poem makes us sympathetically aware of the differences and limitations of pagan ethics and philosophy.

In the same vein, but with less detail, Morton Bloomfield (1952) analyses Chaucer's unusually highly developed historical sense and awareness of cultural difference. He demonstrates that Chaucer was acutely aware of how customs, practices and beliefs differed across time and distance and was sympathetic to such contrasts and variations. Despite some ignorance about the actual practices of pagans, Chaucer blends the contemporary and antique or foreign with intelligence and tact. Bloomfield (1957) also shows Chaucer balancing distance and proximity. He stresses the compulsion to follow historical fact, arguing that the story is in effect pre-destined because Chaucer/the narrator takes it from an authoritative source and cannot alter the events of the tale. Bloomfield believes Chaucer to be as much of a predestinarian as a medieval Christian could be, and finds Troilus closely approaching the narrator's viewpoint in his speech on pre-destination and again at the end. Chaucer, as a Christian, can withdraw from the pagan position to the contemplation of God. Larry Sklute (1984) also identifies the alternation between proximity to and distance from the characters as a means by which Chaucer develops irony or engages the reader in the action. He gives as examples the unnecessary narratorial intervention achieved by breaking the action to divide Books II and III, and the absence of a proem to Book V, forcing the reader into painful proximity to Troilus' suffering. David Wallace (1985) finds in Chaucer's and Boccaccio's treatments of the pagan world not an attempt at fusion or an ironic juxtaposition, but rather a desire 'to explore the uncertain space between [pagan and Christian]. (It was to further such an exploration, Lewis suggests, that Chaucer turned to Boethius.)' This 'encourages us to admire the high moral integrity of pagan protagonists in their simultaneous pursuit of love and truth...such admiration for the "shadowy perfection" of the pagans...brings us into contact with one of the more generous aspects of late medieval thought.'

Lollius, Boccaccio & Co.

Chaucer's use of his sources has been studied in more ways than simply to uncover the elements of medievalising or paganising adaptation in his verse. The principal source for *Tr*, Boccaccio's *Il Filostrato*, has understandably received the most attention, but the inclusion of passages from other works by Boccaccio, and the influence of Boethius, Dante, Statius, Guido delle Colonne, *Le Roman de la Rose* and other writers and works have provided ample scope for source study. Chaucer's professed use of a fictional source, Lollius, gives him, as David Lawton (1983) has noted, complete freedom to use his source material as he wishes without incurring a charge of dishonest representation. But source study is only valuable in so far as it can help us to understand what Chaucer achieves in his particular re-working of the story material. This requires close comparison with the sources, but also analytical thought about the changes we find. Those critics who discuss the ways in which Chaucer has altered the balance of pagan and Christian, medieval and archaic elements clearly make useful comparisons between *Tr* and its sources. Others are less analytical, offering little in the way of new thought, and are useful primarily in preparing the ground. One such study is Sanford B. Meech's long and thorough comparison of *Tr* and *Il Filostrato* (1959). He pays close attention to detail, piling up evidence of changes Chaucer made to all areas of the Italian material. He compares details of social presentation, setting, time, imagery and characterisation, but ultimately draws few conclusions from his mass of material besides the rather general recognition that Chaucer expanded the scope and philosophical content of the story. David Wallace (1985) makes a more constructive comparison. His detailed textual work demonstrates Chaucer's complete understanding of Boccaccio's poetic language, showing how Chaucer changed the Italian at the most minute level of sentence structure and choice of vocabulary. He uses Nick Haveley's translation of *Il Filostrato* (1980) to furnish examples of errors Chaucer avoided, a convincing, though ungenerous, technique.

Chaucer's borrowing extends well beyond Boccaccio, of course. James Lyndon Shanley (1939) finds Chaucer turning to Boethius for the material which gives *Tr* its philosophy. For Shanley, *Tr* is more profound than *Il Filostrato* because Chaucer makes Criseyde a character worthy of love, and focuses on Troilus' fault in misplacing his trust in happiness rather than following Boccaccio in concentrating on the fickleness of women. The influence of Boethius on Chaucer is now well recognised and extensively treated.

James Wimsatt (1979) compares *Tr* with *Le Roman de la Rose*, arguing that both poems share affiliations with contemporary treatises on the art of love (*artes amandi*) and with cosmic allegories (such as the *Consolation of Philosophy*). The practicality, carnality and realism of both poems can be traced to the *artes* (with which Machaut and Froissart had no dealings), while the *Tr* and *Le Roman* are less bawdy and more humane than the *artes amandi*, partly on account of their relation to the cosmic allegories and their use of a Platonic scheme. He thinks it likely that Chaucer deliberately followed the model of *Le Roman* in using the *artes* and cosmic allegories together in a single work. Charles Muscatine also finds similarities between *Le Roman* and *Tr*, arguing that by using Pandarus as an intermediary who allows serious reflection on courtly love, Chaucer was borrowing a technique from Jean de Meun, and combining elements of romance and fabliau tradition. Winthrop Wetherbee (1984) also sees the influence of *Le Roman de la Rose* in Pandarus' role and in the development of the psychology of romance.

Chauncey Wood (1984) begins his book with a critique of *Il Filostrato* which aims to show that its intention, the stance of the narrator, and subsequently the work's treatment of love, are all ironic and that Chaucer recognised and employed this irony. Wood also argues from *Le Roman de la Rose* that love is not, in fact, inescapable – Troilus could have fled from love, though he cannot hope to defeat love once he makes himself vulnerable. (Looking at women seems to constitute contributory negligence.) Wood identifies good and bad love (Troilus' is bad, but he confuses it with the Venus who represents marriage and the love which binds creation), and relates them to the portrayal of erotic and spiritual love in the works of Boccaccio, Boethius and Dante as well as in *Le Roman*.

Guido delle Colonne's version of the Troy story has rarely been cited as a source of Chaucer's poem, but C. David Benson (1980) argues that Chaucer adopted the 'deep pessimism and unusual narrative stance' of Guido's *History of the Destruction of Troy*. He finds *Tr* permeated by an awareness of the Trojan war which is not present in *Il Filostrato*. He sees Chaucer and Guido finding the same fatalistic message in the story – that 'man is fundamentally ignorant and unable to foresee the consequences of his actions'. Benson disputes the extent of free will generally afforded the characters by critics, seeing the operation of fate as a more significant feature than has often been thought recently. He contends that Troilus is aware of the ideal Boethian advice to trust in eternal rather than temporal things, but finds such an answer of little help practically.

Several critics have identified material borrowed from Dante's *Divina Comedia*, most notably Howard Schless (1985). One of the more interesting is Bonnie Wheeler's view (1982) that the abortive attempts at closure and the temptation for the reader to make inappropriate categorical judgments are related to Chaucer's use of material borrowed from Dante in the epilogue. Winthrop Wetherbee (1984) points out that though Troilus' experience is modelled on Dante's progress in the *Comedia*, the allusions to Dante's work undercut Troilus' achievement and reveal its limitations.

An attempt by R.A. Pratt (1956) to demonstrate that Chaucer used a French translation of Boccaccio's poem, *Le Roman de Troyle*, originally earned some credence but has since been substantially discredited. Barry Windeatt (1979) has disputed Chaucer's use of the text, and recent detailed comparison of the Italian and English poems has demonstrated conclusively that Chaucer used Boccaccio's text. It remains possible that he may have used *Le Roman de Troyle* as well, though it so closely resembles the Italian that little conclusive or important evidence is likely to emerge.

Troilus, Criseyde and Pandarus: Psyches, Symbols or Voices?

When Kittredge (1915) called *Tr* the 'first novel, in the modern sense', he initiated an anachronistic way of reading characters and plot. His interpretation of the characters, as psychologically realistic figures interacting dramatically, has had widespread and long-lasting influence. Character studies along the psychological-realism line are still being written. Yet this is not the only way of looking at the characters. Other readers have found symbolic roles more important, and some have found their individuality to be rhetorical – located in different poetic styles and voices – rather than psychological.

Of the early critics, Kittredge and Lewis in particular made pertinent observations about the characteristics of the central figures, many of which have become commonplaces: Criseyde is fearful but practically minded; Troilus fatalistic and ineffectually idealistic; Pandarus a scheming, practical busybody.

Psychological readings of the characters look for plausible motivations, actions developing logically from character and any developments following a natural and credible pattern. For example, Lewis' well-argued case for Criseyde's character being underpinned by fear (of Greeks, of solitude, of treason, of betrayal, of loss of independence) makes her ultimate betrayal of Troilus plausible, if not actually acceptable. Lewis sees no great disparity between her character at the start of the poem and her final actions; though the nature of her actions may change, the character traits which motivate them do not. A critic less sympathetic to the love theme reads the characters very differently. Chauncey Wood (1984) sees Criseyde morally reduced by love as she abandons her scruples in the face of Pandarus' conniving. She is not only fearful but lacks prudence; Troilus is morally and spiritually blind; Pandarus is an evil and scheming destroyer of virtue.

While the same character traits have been generally recognised, they are differently interpreted by different critics. Pandarus for Lewis is a practical busybody but for Wood is a manipulative schemer – the difference lies in the perception of his intentions. Of course, almost all critics of *Tr* discuss the characters and it is not possible here to consider all their conclusions. We shall concentrate instead on the diversity of approaches to the issue of characterisation, rather than enumerating the features each critic has identified. (Alice Kaminsky (1980) covers fully the different readings of each of the characters.)

Some critics have found that inadequacies in the presentation of the psychology of the characters may be accounted for by subordinating the role of character *per se* to other concerns in the poem. This is not the same as finding a different function in the characterisation. Arthur Mizener (1939) locates Chaucer's primary interest in the action, and finds character subordinated to plot. He sees the characters as fixed; for example, we need not see Criseyde as either changing or potentially fickle throughout, her reactions are at every stage those which would be expected of a woman of her nature in the situations in which she finds herself. The question of how the woman of the fixed character whom he sees in Criseyde comes to find herself in such positions (since she acts through her own volition) does not arise, since the demands of the narrative are taken to be paramount and pre-eminent. As

Chaucer could not change events, he does not need to make them emerge naturally from the characters he creates. Rather similar is Elizabeth Salter's view (1966) that inappropriate and inconsistent elements in the characters' behaviour are compensated for by the thematic continuity they serve.

Others find the characterisation important, but do not consider it primarily an attempt at creating plausible individuals. David Aers (1980), finds the poem 'portrays individual consciousness and the relation between Criseyde and Troilus in a mode which incorporates relevant social and ideological dimensions'; it is Criseyde's 'social heritage as a woman (not as a morally weak or oddly timid individual)' that produces her actions. Monica McAlpine (1978) sees in *Tr* not strings of characteristics which account for events, but temperaments or dispositions which, though fixed themselves, do not fix events: the will remains free and unpredictable. We are not able to examine an action in itself, only the change it causes. We cannot know why Criseyde changes, only that her action manifests her freedom. McAlpine rejects all fateful reasoning, demanding that we accept the freedom of the act, and arguing that it is the 'mystery' of freedom and fate that interests Chaucer, and that he explores human freedom through his depiction of character. We are not encouraged to judge the characters, and should avoid treating Criseyde as a possession, or a symbol, or only in relation to other characters. Robert Payne (1963) reads the characters as fixed, conventional types. This prevents us fully empathising with them, and we can therefore retain a more objective view. However, our interpretation of the types alters with the circumstances, so the quality that at one time seems to be integrity later becomes insistent blindness (Troilus), and worldly wisdom is exposed as 'foolishly adaptive evasion of issues' (Pandarus).

Some critics consider the characters to be used symbolically. Wood (1984) sees threads of imagery and associations which reveal personal attributes. Troilus is linked throughout the poem with moral and spiritual blindness which is eventually physically manifested when he mistakes a cart for Criseyde. Criseyde is not only fearful, but lacks prudence (as the heroine says herself) and freely turns away from her moral scruples at Pandarus' practically motivated prompting. Pandarus, in turn, is manipulative and the archetypal 'Evil Counsellor'. The affirmation of the Christian's rightful devotion to God at the end of the text is the culmination of indications built up throughout the poem that Troilus is misguided and sinful. Donald Rowe (1976) also finds much evidence of symbolic significance in the characterisation. Troilus represents the soul and Criseyde the mutable world in a 'sacramental' reading of the action. She incorporates an image of the divine which Troilus perceives, and though the world can distract the soul from God it can also lead back to God. Criseyde is further associated with Fortune and Venus, and in Pandarus too we recognise the intermediary function of Fortune, Venus and Fate. Troilus represents charity and Criseyde cupidity, which in their union create the universe and are 'proof of the stable source of all things'. Similarly, D.W. Robertson (1962) sees in the changes wrought in Troilus by his love 'the results of a moral process, not the operations of psychology'.

For Muscatine, too, the characters have a symbolic dimension, though he relates the poem to literary tradition rather than spiritual experience. Troilus represents a 'courtly, idealistic view of experience' constructed according to courtly stylistic conventions. Pandarus meanwhile provides a 'view of courtly love under the aspect of realism', and the two together generate irony and a reflection on courtly love. Criseyde represents 'earthly instability', and the narrator's professions of ignorance and his sympathy add ambiguity to her presentation. His loyalty mitigates her sin, and allows us to see not a personal weakness but something 'pathetic, universally human'. She is neither a calculating woman nor an innocent betrayed by the treachery of others, but combines elements of both. She has a dual role as woman in danger and as beloved, and is treated in different ways – idolised by Troilus, but treated informally and familiarly by Pandarus. This duality is central, for 'her ambiguity is her meaning'. The symbolic function of the characters is stressed towards the end of the poem as the importance of events and characters fades and the war and the narrator intrude more. This shift focuses our attention on the symbolic element, reducing the importance of the psychological.

A rather different approach to the elucidation of character is used by Ian Bishop (1980). Through close reading of the text he establishes personal vocabularies for each of the characters and demonstrates how other characters are able consciously to use, appropriate or subvert these to communicate effectively or to undermine each other. The individual poetic styles of Troilus and Criseyde (his unrealistic and lyrical, hers practical, crafty, non-imaginative) are also isolated by Rowe, who sees Pandarus able to adopt either as he mediates. Troilus is sullied by union with Criseyde, though she is ennobled by union with him, and their styles come close together, and are even interchangeable, at the point of consummation. Robert Payne (1963) roots the different styles of each character in the rhetorical tradition. He finds Chaucer linking each character's style to their relation to the love theme, so that Troilus' is elaborate and decorative, Pandarus' sententious, and Criseyde's simple and unadorned.

The Narrator and the Poet; Chaucer and the Poets; the Poet and the Text

Is the narrator an important fourth 'character'? Over the years a complex picture of the narrator's character has been built up: he may be in love with his heroine, he certainly tries to skirt the issue of her guilt, he is inexperienced in love himself, abrogates responsibility for his text at difficult moments, and he perhaps responds naively to his own tale. But some critics dispute the existence of a narratorial character at all. Elizabeth Salter (1966) hears only the poet's own voice. The difficulties in the tone, in the sympathy with Criseyde and reluctance to tell a painful story all reflect difficulties Chaucer personally had with the material. These difficulties resulted from the new type of presentation of character that he was attempting in *Tr*; the demands of psychological realism caused their own problems of the poet's relation to the text. Chaucer, unable fully to realise or articulate the discoveries he made in the course of the poem, was forced to end it, making 'all clear, in a description and a reading of life inevitably at odds with his subtler perceptions', a need which resulted in the crisis of the ending.

Others find a partially present or semi-developed narrator. David Lawton (1983) agrees that the role of the narrator has been overstated, though he distinguishes between Chaucer in his normal – what we could call social – role and the voice of the poet in performance. He finds all comments by the narrator-persona suitable to the moment (though they often – and rightly – do not take account of how later events will alter our perception). The same voice narrates throughout, and there is no return to Chaucer's 'own' voice in the epilogue. The many different tones and facets of the narrator-persona are a constant index to the poem's process and performance, and allow simultaneous invocation of a variety of responses. The audience is drawn into participation and relationship to the text by sharing response and wisdom with the narrator-persona, though sometimes the 'I' of the text is incidental, clichéd, and not intended to interpolate a persona. Lawton sees little irony, and none created by a 'gap' between the narrator's pronouncements and the author's real opinions. Each comment is suitable to the moment, and any shifts are appropriate to the poem's process and performance. He argues against finding a narrator who can be extracted from the text and analysed: rhetorical contrivance must remain the domain of the poet, and cannot be attributed to an 'unreliable' narrator, while if the narrator is reliable, there is little rhetorically to distinguish him from the voice of the poet in performance. The narrator-persona's professions of ignorance and his limited sense of his own authority leave us free to judge action and characters if we wish, challenging us to find our own response using our own moral values and selecting from the many tones of the poem. Despite a lucid refutation of Kittredge, Lewis and Donaldson's views of a narrator who refuses to condemn Criseyde, Lawton doesn't successfully locate the narrating voice. It is, he says, 'the voice of an apocryphal author commenting on his own com- position' – but what *is* a narrator character if not an 'apocryphal author'?

Those who discern a narratorial character can locate difficulties in the ending within that character, or can find spiritual enlightenment in his character at the end. E. Talbot Donaldson (1970) charts the narrator's progress in attempting to end the work. As with other Chaucerian narrators, meaning emerges between the narrator's naive pronouncements and the evidence of the text. The narrator in *Tr*, caught up in the beauty of the love-affair, forgets the inevitable ending and is then unable to cope adequately with it. The 'moralitee' which the story must present is inadequate: 'human love, and by a sorry corollary everything human, is unstable and illusory'. But 'the meaning of the poem is not the moral, but a complex qualification of the moral'. In response to the inadequacy of the moral, the narrator goes through various stages of panic-stricken searching for a meaning. He tries epic, moralization, renunciation of responsibility, and joking. Ultimately he enthusiastically launches into the condemnation he had avoided, but the love for the world which previously kept him from that stance permeates and qualifies it. The vanity of temporal concerns is recognised, but they are also necessary and inevitable. The world and heaven grow further apart as he looks at them but are also united in the 'common bond of his love'. It is clear that Donaldson recognises the same issues and difficulties in the text as Salter; the only difference is in Salter's attribution of them to Chaucer and Donaldson's displacement onto a fictional character.

Rowe, too, finds the narrator becoming deeply involved with his story. Beginning from detachment and an overview of the action, he becomes subjective and involved, following the pattern of Troilus' experience. At the end the narrator again moves away to an objective position from which he can place the poem, and learns that poetry must lead men to God through contemplation of the temporal world. This is similar to the view of Wetherbee, who sees the narrator trapped, with Troilus, by a limited, courtly view of love. At the end of the story, however, he is prompted by Troilus' response to look beyond the realm of the poem and is able to see the eternal and spiritual possibilities of love. During the course of the action, Pandarus takes over the role which is rightly the narrator/poet's in organising and orchestrating the action. The narrator, like Troilus, is devoted to the exploration of spiritual fulfilment and is disappointed when it is both achieved and limited in physical consummation. Wetherbee sees the consummation passage as hollow, marked by expressions of inarticulacy.

For Larry Sklute (1984) the inconclusiveness of the ending results directly from the two unintegrated functions of the narrator. The narrator is both a historian trying to get his plot right and an 'actor in the experience of rendering that plot' who is drawn by his involvement to alter it. (C. David Benson (1980) sees a similar dual role for the narrator, as historian and as human being involved in the suffering he must relate, and traces it to the narrative stance in Guido delle Colonne's *History of the Destruction of Troy* (see p. 155 above).) For Sklute, the presence of the narrator is so intrusive as to prevent us reading the poem as a story told by an author with an objective overview. Instead, we are forced to see it as a subjective narrative mediated by a character with limited perception who moulds our responses so that they mirror his own. There is a tension between the objective facts of the source (Lollius) and what they require of the narrator, and his own subjective desires. The tension is not resolved, but is rendered irrelevant by a dual ending, which first fulfils the expectations of the plot and then undercuts the first 'ending' and the values of the poem.

Winthrop Wetherbee (1984) argues that the poem both works out and builds on Chaucer's own perceived relationship with the *poetae* in an attempt to form a valid vernacular continuation of their work. This view is strongly linked to the narrator's role as a story-teller, deriving his material from authoritative sources and becoming involved with the material of the tale itself. The narrator's (or perhaps Chaucer's) involvement with poetic tradition ends with a recognition of his debt to it as well as a new perspective on it. Wetherbee traces a change in the narrator's relation to his material which echoes Chaucer's relation to medieval and Classical tradition. After his involvement with Troilus' story he has separated himself from the pagan tale and 'set it in a larger context that transforms its significance...[it] can now be seen as bearing a typological relation to the narrator's own experience in creating it, an experience that has culminated in the discovery of religious truth'. But it is not necessarily the case that Chaucer's findings about his own relation to the *poetae* are fully communicated in the poem.

Robert Jordan (1967) divides the ending between Chaucer's 'real' voice and the narrator. He divides *Tr*'s structure into three vertical layers. The plot exists on the lowest plane, and is laid out 'horizontally' following a Pythagorean model of multiple distinct elements. The narrator inhabits a plane above this with comment, commentary and assessment of the narrative. The final plane is Chaucer's, and only appears at the end of the poem when he 'steps from behind his mask'. Although the flippancy of the narrator and his comments distract from and clash with the story, the 'interpolations' are as important a part of the poem as the story itself ('the poem is about the teller as well as about the tale he narrates'). The narrator is responsible for the poem up to the dispatch of the book, but it is Chaucer who steps forward to claim it as his book, give it the name of tragedy, and commend himself to God.

As the poet (narrator) takes leave of his texts, questions about its form, substance, relation to past literature and to the future are made explicit. At the end of the poem, Chaucer calls the work a tragedy and dispatches it to go and sit on the steps of great literary endeavour in the company of Classical authors. This literary self-consciousness invites us to consider Chaucer's relationship with the poets of antiquity and his own text, and has proved fertile soil for recent critics. Two important studies take up the reference to the poem as a tragedy, treating it in different ways. J.M. Steadman (1972) devotes a whole book to the development of the literary tradition of apotheosis, trying to place Troilus' experience in the context of other flight motifs in Classical and medieval literature. He finds the *contemptus mundi* theme of Troilus' experience to be common to all flight sequences and argues that it fulfils the Boethian philosophy which has inspired the entire poem. Whereas Boccaccio concentrated on the lesser issue of Creseida's infidelity and unworthiness, Chaucer ends the poem by asserting the value of the 'true' good over the 'false' good of cupidinous love, and rejecting fragile, profane love in favour of divine love.

The *contemptus mundi* theme can be a difficult issue: if the value of what Troilus has lost is denied, our view that his loss is tragic is called into question. Monica McAlpine (1978) takes up this point, investigating the poem's claim to tragic status. She postulates that Chaucer rejects *de casibus* tragedy as incompatible with Boethian philosophy, since it demands an acknowledgment of value in the worldly goods which are to Boethius false and vain (though a common misreading of the *Consolation of Philosophy* does have Boethius consider the loss of worldly bliss tragic). She redefines Boethian tragedy as 'the inner degradation of a person caused by the free commission of an evil act; the punishment for that act is inherent in the act itself'. She finds Chaucer fully aware of the limitations of *de casibus* tragedy and its essentially untragic nature. The narrator erroneously tries to fit Troilus' experience to this pattern, but the tale ultimately transcends tragedy. Troilus gains enlightenment through his love and so is brought closer to man's true goal: his tale is essentially comic; only Criseyde's, with her freely chosen wrong act, is truly tragic. Although we, and the narrator, expect a conclusive ending, it is not appropriate. The poem finishes with several abortive attempts at closure (the end of Troilus and Criseyde's love story; the end of their mortal and immortal careers; the 'definitive' interpretation of the material and the end of the narrator's role as story-teller); but our knowledge of human experience is too limited to allow a conclusive judgment of any kind. She sees in the endings which 'sputter out' 'Chaucer's belief that it is impossible or unprofitable to draw large morals from the fraction of human experience any work of art can represent'. The ending is appropriate in that the narrator signals the end of his involvement, leaves the work to posterity, his material to further treatments and admits his inadequacy. It is also important, she says, because it approaches 'the making of an ending as an issue'.

Larry Sklute (1984) also discusses the sequences of endings and the status of the poem as a tragedy. He finds the first ending conclusive, fulfilling the expectations of the plot, but the second undercutting the moral message and values of the poem. The second ending is totally reductive, denying the validity of all that the poem has discussed. Sklute interprets it as an over-reaction on the part of the narrator to the insufficiency he sees in the first ending. As tragedy, he says, *Tr* has no hint of hope, no acknowledgement of man's power and nobility. It undercuts our sense of the genre, and implies that tragedy would not be possible in a Christian universe.

Chapter 4

'Such stuff as dreams are made on':
The *Book of the Duchess*, the *House of Fame*, the *Parliament of Fowls* and the *Legend of Good Women*

Chaucer's interest in the dream form lasted nearly 25 years, from the *Book of the Duchess* (*BD*, *c.* 1370) to his final revision of the *Legend of Good Women* (*LGW*, 1394). One of the form's attractions, no doubt, was the freedom it allowed him. A dream-poem is not bound to conform to the logic of causality, it does not have to be plausible, and it does not need an explicit narrative sequence. These same features make the poems slippery for critics. Like the whirling wicker house of Rumour, it is not clear how we get in. We tend to think of Chaucer as a story-teller, but here there is little sequential plot. Elsewhere we might admire his characterisation, but the only real character in these poems – the dreamer – is elusive. The poems consequently enjoyed little respect until the middle of the 20th century, and even more recently have still been variously dismissed as early experiments, incoherent collections of jumbled episodes, or occasional pieces which cannot be fully understood without recourse to lost historical data. But it is perhaps the dream-poems which should appeal most strongly to the more authentically modern of modern readers. In them Chaucer explores, more explicitly than any other writer for several centuries after him, the process of the creative imagination and the role of the writer in relation to his literary heritage.

An Overview

Early criticism of the dream-poems concentrated on personal or historical allegory and on seeking Chaucer's literary sources. The obscure narratives of the dream-poems seem to make them good candidates for historical-allegorical treatment, and many critics have thought them to be occasional pieces, perhaps commissioned, to commemorate court events. Some useful information has been uncovered, both early on and later in the search. It is now generally accepted that *BD* was written for John of Gaunt after the death of his first wife Blanche in 1368, although the poem's date is still disputed. The occasion of the *Parliament of Fowls* (*PF*) was for a long time taken to be the betrothal of Richard II to Anne of Bohemia, though other engagements have been suggested. The *House of Fame* (*HF*) does not obviously relate to any particular event, though some critics have thought the 'man of gret auctoritee' would deliver some court gossip, slander or announcement. Alceste's command that Chaucer write *LGW* and deliver the finished poem to the queen has led some to infer a real commission. The concern with historical occasions has largely passed out of vogue. This is no bad thing, since finding the event a poem commemorates rarely gives us much insight into the quality (or indeed meaning) of the poem itself. The event of Blanche's death may set the limits of court decorum within which *BD* probably operates, but knowing the occasion is otherwise of little help in understanding the poem, and the same is probably true of the other dream-poems.

Another phase in criticism which has largely passed is the assumption that the narratorial persona and Chaucer the poet are one and the same person. This approach finds reflected in the events of the dream-poems (such as they are) real details about the life and character of the poet. So if Geffrey in *HF* has a nagging wife, we are to take this as an indication that Chaucer's own marital relations were less than satisfactory. Not only is this a naive reading of the poems, it further makes Chaucer undiplomatic enough to risk enraging a nagging wife by parading her faults before the whole court! What we discern of Chaucer himself in the dream-poems is not in the caricatured presentation of the poet in the narratorial persona, but in the concerns and difficulties he examines in the poems, particularly those relating to his creativity and his role as a poet.

A more sophisticated and productive approach to the dream-poems developed with New Critical close-reading techniques. These made the surface texture of the poems meaningful and gave new insight into Chaucer's use of and allusions to sources and literary tradition. Concentrating on form and the character of the narrator, critics began to explore such questions as: what type of unity can be found in the structure of the poems? how does the narrator figure contribute to each poem's meaning? and how did Chaucer see his own work in relation to his predecessors? Readers discussed the issues which the poems raise explicitly – particularly love, but also fame, politics, poetic activity and philosophical questions. Later, the allegorical readings of the Robertsonian school of Chaucer criticism in the 1960s found Christian charity and salvation uncovered by exegetical techniques.

One of the important areas of investigation was in the combination of dream realism and literary tradition. The most comprehensive work in this field is by Constance B. Hieatt (1967), who finds Chaucer preferring the structures and patterns of actual dreams to the poetic conventions. Where he does use the conventions of dream-poetry, they are rendered plausible and realistic; so the traditional dream landscape of *BD* is part of the dreamer's waking literary experience which credibly reappears in his dream. Briefer introductions to dream theory are given by A.C. Spearing (1976) and James Winny (1973). Others concentrate on literary models. Dorothy Bethurum (1959) identifies the narrator's character both allowing a parody of the love-vision form and reducing the usual immediacy of the emotional impact, especially in *BD* where he 'filters' the Black Knight's experience. James Winny finds Chaucer rejecting the static picture of idealised life, the allegorical portrayal of courtly ideas and the social limitation of the French poems, and Piero Boitani (1982) sees him greatly extending the scope of the dream-vision to cover 'everything that is susceptible of poetic resonance and attention, including poetry itself'.

Other elements of style have also been related to literary tradition. Charles Muscatine (1957) sees Chaucer learning how to combine the realistic and the allegorical modes, returning to the model of *Le Roman de la Rose* and its successful combination of real experience and allegorical expression. Patricia Kean (1972) describes the development of Chaucer's urbane, conversational style and absorption of other poetic voices from English and foreign tradition to forge his own poetic language, and Robert Payne (1963) finds the dream-poems combining elements of experience, authority and dream, and demonstrating the paradox of art's claims to reorder knowledge and experience.

Recently the critical ground has shifted again: the concepts of unity and coherent characterisation have become mis-readings imposed, in Jordan's view (1987), by an anachronistically realist mentality on poems which are in effect a collage (one senses an echo of Derrida's *bricolage*) of rhetorical blocks 'patched' together. The best recent criticism of the poems has found wider epistemological problems behind the questions explicitly posed. The poems have been shown to be dealing with the nature of knowledge, memory, the creative imagination and language. The most exciting developments in the 1970s and 1980s have been in this direction. But sometimes the texture and tone are overlooked by those who dig deep, and we can sense a considerable disparity between what a critic finds a poem to be saying and how we feel it communicates with us.

The Book of the Duchess

The book and the duchess

The historical event which lies behind *BD* is the only one which can be identified with any certainty in relation to the poem. In some senses, knowing the occasion has restricted criticism, and as late as 1952, Bertrand Bronson found it necessary to demonstrate that the conventional courtliness of the Black Knight and his wife is not a failure to represent the characters of Gaunt and Blanche accurately but is deliberate. It has been common to assume that a certain attitude should be discerned in the dreamer's behaviour, or that there can be no criticism of the Black Knight, because we would expect Chaucer to treat his patron's bereavement with tact and decorum. Even Bronson thought the Black Knight's elegy balanced intimacy with Chaucer's knowledge to produce words suitable for John of Gaunt. But the poem is not only an elegy for Blanche. If it were, the Black Knight's account of his love and loss could stand alone. Other concerns of *BD* which have been put forward include a more general exploration of love and death; the presentation of a narratorial character who may or may not be changed by his experience; Chaucer's interest in the similarity of the creative process in dreaming and in writing poetry; or a demonstration of the poet in action. None of these is linked with the historical event the poem commemorates. As an independent work of art, which can be profitably read without historical knowledge of the Duke's loss, the poem is a greater monument to Blanche than a conventional memorial poem could ever have been, and to do the poem justice, we must free BD from the shadow of the duchess.

The book and the dreamer

The nature of the dreamer's character is perhaps the most contentious issue in the poem. Some early critics took him to be more or less a representation of Chaucer himself. Later critics maintained a split between poet and narrator to differing extents, ranging from Kittredge's view (1915) that he is 'a purely imaginary figure, to whom certain purely imaginary things happen, in a purely imaginary dream' to Bronson's view (1952) that he is a shifted version of Chaucer himself, and not a wholly fictitious character. Most recently, his 'character' has slipped out of focus, with his structural role commanding more attention.

Once we have accepted that the narrator has an independent existence, character analysis becomes a possible route into BD and its meaning. Accounts of the narrator's character are widely divergent. He has been seen as both tactful and obtuse, as an unhappy lover and a sinner wallowing in worldliness. In character analyses the main points of dispute are the nature of his eight years' sickness at the start of the poem and whether he understands the cause of the Black Knight's sorrow when he overhears his lament. If he does not understand the lament, he must be 'almost unimaginably stupid'; if he does, is he being tactful in prompting the Black Knight into a therapeutic catharsis, or intrusive in curiously probing his sorrow? The answers seem to depend in part on how we interpret his sickness. If it is love-sickness, it becomes possible that the dreamer's curiosity is aroused rather than his compassion. If it is not love-sickness, can we say what troubles him?

Kittredge (1915), responding to critics who considered the dreamer impossibly stupid, or Chaucer incompetent in letting him overhear something he promptly forgets, saw the dreamer as childlike and naive, artless and sympathetically curious, but at the same time aware of the reason for the Black Knight's sorrow. But long after Kittredge, others have continued to see him characterised by, in Stephen Manning's inelegant phrase 'nonpareil dullwittedness' (1956). The narrator has had various champions to defend him from the charge of stupidity, though they disagree on his motives and the effectiveness of his treatment of the Knight.

Bronson (1952) finds the dreamer pretending not to know of White's death because he should not have overheard the Black Knight's lament. Clemen (1963) agrees that the dreamer fakes misunderstanding in order to bring consolation to the Knight through allowing him to recreate his past, but 'death overwhelms him anew with its relentless finality'. Patricia Kean (1972) also sees the narrator as tactful, giving the Black Knight the opportunity for a therapeutic exploration of his grief: he is temporarily cut off from life by his grief, but he can rejoin society at the end of the poem. John Lawlor (1956) disregards any sympathetic motivation, and takes the dreamer for an unsuccessful lover prompted by curiosity to discover the extent of the Black Knight's misfortune. Charles Muscatine (1957) has it both ways, fusing the dreamer's experience as a lover with his compassionate tact, saying that his own experience prompts him to over-eager questioning which brings a surprising and awkward realism.

Some readers have found the tact required of the dreamer for a therapeutic function is too great, but reject the view that he is stupid. Instead they try to work around the problem of the lament by making his structural function paramount or arguing that the misunderstanding is plausible. A.C. Spearing (1976) has the dreamer not actually overhearing the lament he later seems to misunderstand, but performing a functional role in *BD* by communicating the lament to the reader. Robert Jordan (1974) shares this view, considering the narrator's structural role more important than his character throughout. W.H. French (1949) and Ruth Morse (1980) both argue that the dreamer might well take the Black Knight's song not as a literal account of his own situation but as suitable to his miserable state. Another approach attributes his inability to understand the Black Knight to the dreamer's narrow vision. John Fyler (1979) sees the dreamer so blinkered by his own sorrow and his certainty that the world is a bad place that he is not receptive to the Black Knight's story. Spearing (1976) finds a clue in modern psychology. He sees the Black Knight as an embodiment of the dreamer's misery, but also sees the dreamer projecting his own problems onto the Black Knight so that he finds it difficult to see the real nature of the Knight's sorrow. Bronson also saw the Black Knight as a projection of the dreamer's sorrow,

with the Black Knight's eulogy discharging the dreamer's guilt at
wishing his own cruel lady dead. James Winny (1973) finds a
comfortable position on the fence. For him, the dreamer combines
elements of sophistication with moments of dullness. He sees in
this an attempt to present a standard dream character challenged
by an impulse to comedy. Chaucer adapts the complaint-and-
comfort pattern by using a narrator not up to the task in hand. The
dreamer seems unable to recognise the Black Knight's state of
mind because he is not familiar with courtly romanticism or ideals,
and *BD* uses this to criticise courtly tradition. The poem
simultaneously shows compassion for the Knight and criticises the
standards of *fin amour*.

For David Lawton (1983), the poem charts the poetic initiation
of the narratorial persona. His involvement with the Black Knight
teaches him by example what it is like to feel strong emotion and
so stirs compassion in him. The development of pity in the narrator
is the important development of the poem. Rather than bringing
consolation (the Black Knight could articulate his sorrow from the
start), the dreamer is enriched and turned into a poet by his
interaction with the Knight, who has an Orphic role. Lawton and
Muscatine see the narratorial persona split, after the fashion of *Le
Roman de la Rose*, into a young dreamer and an older poet
recasting the experience. Boitani sees the development from one
to the other, with the poet actually maturing during the course of
the poem so that 'it seems in fact to create its own author'.

Finally, there are critics who reject the whole concept of a
characterised narrator. The fragmentation of the narrator is
perhaps a step towards this. Jordan (1974, 1987) sees the
narrator's structural role as predominant: 'the dreamer's
transitional function overrides his dramatic function or characterization' (1987). He is not a 'unified consciousness' but instead
maintains 'narrative momentum', taking on the traits and role
necessary at any moment (1974).

The book and the dream: unity and structure
As we have seen, some critics have seen a development in the
narrator which unites the parts of the poem. But many of the
discussions mentioned above neglect much of the poem,
concentrating solely on the dream element.

There is a clear parallel between the situations of Alcyone and the Black Knight, as Bronson pointed out, but other elements are not as clearly linked, and the structure of the poem seems disjunct. Early critics detected the ineptitude of an immature and inexperienced poet in *BD*'s diverse parts; but most recently, this structure has been thought deliberate and crucial to the poem's meaning. If we take our cue from the critics, we can either accept this disjunction or seek a unifying principle for the poem. Attempts to find a unifying principle in the poem have ranged from thematic or philosophical interpretations through dramatic to structural or formal studies. Reading the parts as a cohesive whole requires finding connections – implicit or explicit – to bridge the divisions of the poem into an expository prologue, a re-telling of Ovid's tale, and the various parts of the dream.

Wolfgang Clemen (1963) set the general pattern for reading the juxtaposed plot elements. He sees connections between the parts left implicit, making of Chaucer's roundabout approach to his themes a more personal statement than explication could allow. For most readers, this is the natural way to read the poem and appears characteristic of Chaucer's mode of composition. Such a method at first suggests that creative juxtaposition, a series of correlative episodes in which each part affects our reading of the others, may be an acceptable account of the poem. But Clemen does not leave it there. He feels the common tendency to find or impose sequence; it is not only the critics but also *BD*'s narrator himself who tries to impose or imply causal links. Clemen found the forward impetus of the poem in postponement; first sleep is postponed, then the Black Knight's statement is postponed so that 'the whole poem appears to exist simply in order to prevent this direct statement from having been made earlier'.

Those readers who find the dreamer maturing, emerging as a poet, or changing in some other way, fit the poem to a sequential pattern. Other readers are happy to allow the juxtaposed elements and the themes they suggest to coexist in harmony or tension, but generally without final resolution. Despite identifying a sequential, creative pattern of book-becoming-dream and dream-becoming-new-book, Boitani (1986) describes the poem as binomial, being constructed around oppositions in which dialogue is the narrative principle: there are parallels of description, and thematic pairs and contrasts (such as literature and reality, dream and book). There is more contrast than unity in the poem, denying the need to resolve the issues into an 'answer'.

Another critic for whom BD is organised around opposites is F.M. Fyler (1979), who sees the narrator's view of the world as fallen contrasted with visions of the Golden Age. First, the narrator cannot understand the tale of Ceyx and Alcyone because it depicts a time when men and women followed Nature's law. Then the narrator misundertands the Black Knight, whose tale images the devotion and nobility of the classical tale. The dreamer uses arguments and exempla suitable only to his own sorrow because he is sure the Golden Age is lost. The poem praises Gaunt and Blanche, as their representatives in the poem demonstrate that such love is still possible and that there is something valuable in preserving the memory of Blanche, who recognised and rejected the inadequacies of the fallen present. Derek Traversi (1987) finds the parts linked by a frustrated attempt to reconcile another pair of opposites, experience and authority. However, the poem discovers the impossibility of applying the rational lessons of authority to personal emotional experience.

Robert Jordan (1974) is another reader who employs the structural role of the narrator as the element which links but does not unify the parts. He offers an 'aesthetic' approach to the poem, explaining that the dreamer's role links eleven distinct structural parts in a 'disjunct, discontinuous narrative mode'. Jordan thinks we should not seek superficial types of unity in the poem: 'The aesthetic principle holding such parts of the poem together is one of accommodation...[rather than] a concept of integration, whether of organic characterization or unified theme'. Jordan (1987) developed this idea further, undoing the types of unity others have seen in the poem. The poem is, he argues, built up of 'narrative blocks' employing various literary forms – 'lyric, narrative, descriptive, didactic and to an extent dramatic' – which form versions of eulogy and consolation held together 'by transitional passages often incongruent in tone and of dubious thematic relevance'.

The search for a structure for experience is a controlling device in R.A. Shoaf's reading of the poem (1981). He finds a pattern for the Black Knight's experience in the transformation of repentance into a story. He argues that the act of interpreting experience in the poem, and our interpretation of the poem, is necessarily one of finding or imposing an appropriate structure. For Shoaf, the Black Knight's sin is in insisting on living in the past, thus betraying both himself (seeing himself in the role of courtly lover or abstractions) and his story by denying it the 'preterite of story': he must fix his experience in the past. The Black Knight must change to find a suitable role for himself, validate his story and transform the nature of his love. He finally does this, having exhausted inappropriate rhetoric, when he admits 'she ys ded'.

Sources, traditions and models

Early critics related *BD* generically to its French models, but James Wimsatt (1968) gives an extended treatment of the French sources and models. He demonstrates Chaucer's indebtedness to *Le Roman de la Rose* and the *dits amoreux*, itemises verbal, thematic and structural influences, and finds *La Fonteinne Amoreuse* the most important source. Elsewhere (1967) he posits that elements of the description of Blanche relate her to the Blessed Virgin. Revisiting the topic in 1981, he notes that this suggests contrasting interpretations: we can follow either the secular French influences on the poem or the religious influences and elements and arrive at different readings. He finds the text consistently ambiguous and without guidance in the matter. It fufils the genre expectations of the complaint-and-comfort poems (especially those of Machaut) and at the same time is a religious vision of the same type as *Pearl* and Dante's *Il Purgatorio*. The poem supports both readings and precludes intelligent choice.

The poem's fluid relationship to familiar literary forms has prompted critics to isolate elements of recognisable genres and examine their use. Clemen (1963) sees Chaucer separating the elements of elegy, presenting the lament and eulogy separately and further reducing the impact of the lament by fitting it into the topos of a love complaint. He finds the style of *BD* more colloquial and realistic than Machaut's, and observes that in the prologue the narrator is very much like a person talking to himself. Patricia Kean (1972) also notices this tone, and finds *BD* developing the urbane style of the short poems. The carefully observed conversational style of the narrator and Knight creates a vivid impression of social contact and interaction. Both critics are identifying features of the style which do not coincide with our expectations of the genre, something which Muscatine (1957) found a problem. He saw a 'strain of realism in the midst of conventional elevation', the style showing movement towards 'a functional use of courtly convention...[and] a realism that suggests comic disenchantment'. Winny (1973) discerns in this disparity between genre expectations and the poem's reality a criticism of courtly tradition and *fin amour*.

R.A. Shoaf (1981) sees the pattern of confession as that which the poem finally fixes on. The dreamer acts as a confessor, drawing out the Knight's story by following in outline the sequence of questions advocated by the penitential manuals. He compares *BD* with Augustine's *Confessions* and *Le Roman de la Rose*, finding confession the most appropriate form for autobiography. The elements of complaint and elegy are less important in the poem than the form of confession and autobiography, forged into the new form of dream autobiography.

The most controversial reading of *BD* comes from Bernard F. Huppé and D.W. Robertson (1963), who approach the poem through the use of exegetical techniques. They find *BD* teaching faith and comfort in Christ, and vary the usual incorporation of the Lancasters into the poem: the narrator is in a miserable torpor because of the death of Blanche, but the Black Knight does not represent Gaunt, nor White the dead duchess. The Ceyx and Alcyone story demonstrates the right attitude towards grief and the dream shows a symbolic awakening to the message of Christ and the hope of the Resurrection. Each stage of the dream and the pre-dream narrative is allocated an allegorical significance. For example, the hunting king Octovyen is Christ pursuing the human soul; the hart that steals away is like the narrator who does not heed God's word. In the dream, the narrator is split in two: the grief-stricken Knight, and a character who knows that comfort comes from Christ and elicits a healing confession from the Knight. White represents spiritual beauty and charity which redeemed the Knight when, in his youth, he had fallen into cupidity. Her virtue guided him, but he is unable to see that her death should bring him closer to Christ since her virtues live on. At the end of the poem the narrator has learnt the way to his Physician.

Consolation and philosophy
There is little agreement about whether the Knight (or the narrator) is finally consoled. If there is consolation, it may be from the

therapeutic activity of talking about the Knight's past (see, for example, Kean, 1972) or may be philosophical. John Lawlor (1956) detects a three stage pattern of consolation. First the dreamer offers the consolation of contempt of Fortune, then the consolation of fulfilment is realised through the Black Knight's description of his life and love, and finally the consolation of understanding comes with the explication and the dreamer's pity. Lawlor suggests that Chaucer follows Machaut in rejecting the inadequacy of traditional response and asserts the force of loss.

Michael Cherniss (1987) finds the poem suffused with Boethian philosophy which patterns its structure and provides the consolation. He compares the role of Boethius' Lady Philosophy with that of the narrator, and Boethius with that of the Black Knight. The poem is about how to deal with misfortune, and endorses the standard Boethian acceptance of the blows of Fortune with a recognition of their absolute (un)importance. That the misery of the narrator has an unspecified cause extends the terms of reference from bereavement to all types of misfortune. The poem is strikingly innovative in that the narrator becomes the authority figure in his own dream, and the dreamer does not benefit from his vision but returns to his former misery on waking. (Cherniss' two earlier articles on the topic (1969, 1972) work towards the conclusions explained in his book, with interesting additional points about the distribution of the Philosophy/Boethius roles between the narrator and Black Knight.)

For Shoaf (1981) consolation is not possible while the Black Knight retains an inappropriate view of his past, trapped in unsuitable rhetoric, and excluding the dreamer by his private language. It can only come when he correctly formulates his past as a story. Until then, the language of *fin amour* obscures his meaning, forces a conventional formulation on his wife, commits him to an inappropriate role and propels him towards suicide. The dream and the Black Knight's narrative represent mutability, and the act of interpretation – finding or imposing a structure – is a natural response to mutability. The finished poem is a 'life-affirming response to death' that makes a meaningful present from the material of the past.

Other critics have discovered no successful consolation at all. For Clemen (1987) grief returns at the end of the poem. Traversi (1987) explores the polarity of authority and experience and finds that the lesson of authority – that love cannot be immortal – can only be accepted in the abstract, it does not ease the pain of loss in individual experience. Although the dreamer's initial torpor and the story of Ceyx and Alcyone both demonstrate the fruitlessness of extended grief and prefigure the misery the Black Knight must shake off, the poem ends without resolution since authority and experience are ultimately irreconcilable. The lesson of authority is essential for a right understanding of life, but experience returns us 'to the finally intractable nature of given reality'. Fichte (1980) thinks the dreamer deliberately unsuited to the task of consolation because the poem is not itself intended as consolation (for Gaunt), but as an encomium for the duchess. The Ceyx and Alcyone story sets the pattern of the finality of death and inconsolability of the bereaved, and the dream endorses this.

The Parliament of Fowls

The parts of *PF* are less clearly linked than those of *BD*. The poem expresses early on a concern with philosophy which does not seem to be sustained, and has an insubstantial plot in which the narrator's involvement is minimal. Perhaps because of these features, critics have looked long and hard for some historical event plausibly celebrated by the poem.

The most commonly cited occasion for the poem is the engagement of Richard II and Anne of Bohemia in 1381. Originally formulated by John Koch, Samuel Moore and O.F. Emerson, between 1911 and 1914, this view has been revived recently by Larry D. Benson (1982). Benson explains that Anne of Bohemia had three suitors when she chose Richard, and that the poem makes it obvious which suitor the formel should choose, thus clearly supporting Richard's case. Edith Rickert (1920) suggested that the royal eagle and formel represented Richard II and Philippa of Lancaster, eldest daughter of John of Gaunt, and Haldeen Braddy (1932) identified them with Richard and Princess Marie of France. Thus each of Richard's attempts at marriage has had its turn. Other, more obscure, identifications have also been suggested. Bertrand Bronson (1948) thought the illogic of the birds' speeches suggested the poem first related to only one suitor, but that Chaucer later revised it to remove it from its historical occasion and make it more interesting.

Attempts to read the poem as historical allegory share one important failing: they tend to concentrate on only the parliament itself – and then on the part played in it by the formel and three eagles. Benson is aware of this deficiency and incorporates the earlier, Ciceronian, concern with good government and 'common profit' by suggesting that the poem as a whole should be seen as a mirror for princes, with the message that it would be good for the country if Richard were to marry and produce an heir. On the whole, though, historical allegory does not accommodate the other parts (the majority) of the poem. Some other methods of approach, too, concentrate on parts rather than the whole, and the central difficulty critics face is in finding a meaning in the poem which explains the link between the Dream of Scipio, the dreamer's tour around the garden, and the love-debate. Some find the parts so incompatible they are forced to reject (or ignore) one or other of them. Thus Bronson (1948) concludes that the garden 'has little organic part in the whole design'. He and Wolfgang Clemen (1963) see *PF* primarily as an occasional poem and assume that this excuses it from the obligation to have a coherent structure or serious point.

'Love in dede' and common profit

Until relatively recently, love was commonly considered the only important issue in *PF*. Thus for Clemen the poem shows contrasting features of love. Through the garden, temple and parliament, Chaucer demonstrates 'the contradictions in Love's whole complex range' first introduced by the message over the gate, which presents not a choice but two possibilities which must be accepted together. The issue at question in the parliament is too clear-cut to arouse much interest, but the debate quickly expands into the wider issue of the variety of attitudes towards love, each of which illuminates the others. The birds represent different social orders which are incapable of understanding each others' attitudes; Clemen sees Chaucer's primary intention to bring the different attitudes to love into 'genially impartial contrast', stimulating critical appraisal.

In the only book-length study of *PF*, J.A.W. Bennett (1957) finds the poem setting out Chaucer's views on love and its relation to Nature. Nature's role is close to her role in the *Anticlaudianus*, but the chain of love is Chaucer's own invention, a compound of ideas from Boethius, Alain de Lille and *Le Roman de la Rose*. The poem shows love, nature and order in accord. As long as love has its end in marriage and 'engendrure' it is natural and good, but illicit love is contrary to nature. Charles Muscatine (1957) finds the comic variety of attitudes towards love the unifying theme of *PF*. The various idealistic and realistic, conventional and naturalistic elements from French tradition are drawn into 'meaningful polarity', Chaucer making more comprehensible order of the legacy of French poetry than his continental contemporaries. For Muscatine, 'the irony of the case, rather than the issues, is the prime consideration', and while the parliament 'cast[s] something of a retrospective coherence' over the earlier part of the poem, the ironic juxtaposition of social attitudes is more important. Like many critics who focus on the parliament, Muscatine is unable to see any serious point to the early part of the poem, dismissing the inclusion of Scipio's dream as 'comic antithesis, a joke at the expense of the Narrator'.

Just as some critics have found love the dominant element, others have focused on the political interest of the parliament and the Dream of Scipio. Bruce Kent Cowgill (1975) sees the poem as a political allegory, moving from aridity towards plenty and the common profit, which is the fulfilment of human potential since 'life in the human community frees [man] from the corrupt selfhood'. The tercel's refusal to take a mate is criticised as perverting Nature's injunction and precipitating disharmony; Venus promotes selfish interest as opposed to common profit. Cowgill sees the lack of leadership which allows the tercel's rebellion as a reference to the Peasants' Revolt. Paul Olson (1980) also sees the poem endorsing human fulfilment in democratic parliamentary procedure. He relates the political thought of the poem to the Aristotelean ideal of the parliament. The idea of common profit is introduced by Scipio's dream but this gives no indication of how to achieve common profit. Venus represents self-interest and 'civic cupidity' which the parliament overcomes with a unified society discovering civic charity. The four estates are presented, with their different approaches to solving the problem, though none is particularly appropriate to the love-match.

Both these approaches – that concentrating on love and that emphasising political thought – run into the perennial difficulty of locating the poem's unity. Some critics have tried to explicate the connection between the love, political and philosophical elements. Their methods vary between showing that one element triumphs over the other, or that the elements exist in harmony, or that the poem closes with unresolved tensions. Constance Hieatt (1967) says that at first there seem to be no meaningful links between the parts, and in this *PF* emulates the logic of real dreams. She goes on to enumerate and explain the hidden links, which are thematic, imaginative and structural. Wolfgang Clemen, though, sees superficial links between the dream of Scipio and the narrator's dream which veil deeper contrasts between the sombre and serious philosophical dream of Scipio and the narrator's realistic and vital dream, with Nature a poetic symbol for conquest over the *contemptus mundi* philosophy of Scipio's dream.

Amongst those who see no successful integration of the parts is Derek Traversi (1987). He argues that *PF* is inconclusive because the traditional philosophy of Nature does not quite gel with the boisterous parliament. (His account includes a lucid introduction to the Platonic premises of the goodness of creation and the principle of plenitude which inform Chaucer's presentation of Nature.) For Charles Owen (1953) this tension represents a deliberate rejection of the philosophy of the early part of the poem, with the narrator turning away from common profit to physical love. This demonstrates 'the small appeal that idealism holds for the inner motivation of most men'. Something similar is suggested by Larry Sklute's conclusion that the dreamer's disappointment with his reading is supported, since the dream questions Macrobius' authority, and the parliament celebrates the carnality Africanus denies; the two parts of the poem are connected only obliquely and through antithesis.

Michael Cherniss (1987) also points out the limitations of Scipio's *Dream*. Chaucer's retelling adjusts the emphasis to incorporate 'love' in the largest sense (so public service is seen as love of common profit), but the *Dream* polarises affairs, setting worldly pleasure against common profit, and does not accommodate love. Thus although Africanus links the cosmic wisdom of Scipio with the narrator's dream, he cannot guide him to love. His dream depicts the mixture of good and bad features of love, and the garden fills in the earthly space between the heaven and hell of Scipio's dream, acknowledging the place of erotic love in Nature's plan of procreation. The parliament represents the range, ambiguity and problems of real earthly love and shows love equally resistant to order, reason and easy comprehensibility, though in taking appropriate mates the birds do serve common profit. The dreamer, a Boethian character searching for something stable (the 'certain thing'), fails to learn that confusion and lack of reason are the nature of love. Similarly, John Fyler (1979) sees the structures man finds in or imposes on the world collapsing as he faces instinctive nature. The narrator struggles 'to disentangle the paradox [of love] in a series of juxtapositions; but he succeeds in creating only a spurious clarity, and the conflicts he exposes are left unresolved'. However, there is life-potential in the consciousness (and fallen-ness) that sets man apart from nature. Joerg Fichte (1980) also sees a frustrated search for certainty and order in which Scipio's model of order proves inadequate. The narrator's confusion is reflected in the affective rhetoric, juxtapositions, transitions and stylistic variety found beneath the ordered surface of the verse. Again the impossibility of reconciliation is demonstrated in R.M. Lumiansky's philosophical reading of the poem (1948). He finds in it a Boethian search for reconciliation between true and false felicity. The poem reflects Chaucer's own unease at being unable to reconcile writing love poems with hoping for bliss in the after-life. The hope of reconciling the two elements is presented dramatically in the mediatory figure of Africanus, but the hope is false.

Other critics find a means of harmonising the concerns of common profit and love. Patricia Kean (1972) sees the poem showing the 'application of the moral-philosophical ideas of Macrobius and Boethius to love in its various aspects'. Unruly and self-indulgent passion breaks the natural law, while love is a unifying and creative force in harmony with common profit. The parliament, though, makes abstract theorising and philosophy irrelevant. While the attitude of the noble birds is at odds with the preferable natural solution, it offers wider scope for experience: 'it is only on reflection that we realize how much light has been thrown on the themes...of contradictory love and common profit'. For Piero Boitani (1982), the poem shifts its definition of love to include all life, art and poetry, and the love of common profit that is finally rewarded: 'Love is the salvation and aggrandisement of the *res publica* – or, in a wider sense, of the whole of mankind'. David Lawton (1983) sees the parts fused by a cumulative process, with the dreamer's vision supplementing the austere and unattractive public vision of Scipio, and giving an acceptable pattern to experience. Both dreaming and art impart order to experience and emotion. Nature 'stands for the kind of order we impose and have to impose on the external world, in order to perceive and in order to think'. The acts of reading and ordering experience produce art and allow the discovery of 'a new, non-penitential value for experience'.

In the allegorical reading of Robertson and Huppé (1963), the vision endorses Scipio's dream. For them, the theme of *PF* is the futility of earthly love. It is set against the 'true love of the seeker of wisdom' and Cicero's world view is approved. The garden is like paradise and is a symbolic depiction of the church as it should be: those who enter in sin will find misery, while those who enter pure will have bliss. There is a polarity between Nature (administering God's natural law for common profit) and the cupidity and self-seeking of Venus. The royal eagle shows himself following the wrongful Venus and the tercel cannot rightly choose him because his motivation is wrong. His selfish attitude frustrates Nature's plan and leads towards insurrection, though Nature cannot see that it is self-seeking which frustrates the parliament. The tercel can make no natural or rational choice and so sterility is inevitable.

Dissonant or harmonious voices?
The poem has many voices, from Scipio's to the birds', all clamouring to be heard and hoping to be authoritative. The cacophony of voices may be set against the narrator's desire for a 'certain [stable] thing', or *PF*'s variety of opinion may be encouraged by his failure to impose a personal view or give priority to any voice he hears. The diversity of opinion expressed in the poem is a virtue in itself: the end effect may be reconciliation of the different voices, or tension between them, or a celebration of pluralism.

John McCall (1979) sees harmony emerging from dissonance, 'interweaving...individual discordances in general accord'. The 'garden of this life' and the parliament show the duality of life and creation, the one iconographically and the other dramatically, but in both discord is finally productive of harmony. To seek for a reconciliation in the poem is misguided because it is the combination of dissonant elements which ultimately produces order and calm. David Lawton (1983) sees the multiplicity of tones and voices in the poem representing the multiplicity of attitudes and resembling the subject matter of the poem. The narrator does not foreclose the perspective, and the different approaches are all allowed to stand. James Winny (1973) agrees that the poem is inconclusive, shelving the debate at the end and containing unresolved conflicts and problems. The undetermined outcome shows Chaucer representing his 'uncertainty in the face of a challenge to his future development as a poet'. Larry Sklute (1981) finds that, taken together, the inconclusiveness and the multiplicity of voices express something more profound and constructive than Chaucer's private worry about his career. The reduced involvement of the narrator, his ambivalence and 'naively limited understanding' contribute to the inconclusiveness of the poem. Although the narrator shies away from complexity in his search for one 'certain thing', Chaucer is denying the possibility of a single definition of love and 'directs our attention to the fact of pluralistic opinion'. In doing this, he undermines authority, asserting the validity of individual opinion.

H.M. Leicester (1974) also relates the issue to authority and the variety of literary tradition. 'In trying to harmonize the materials of his dream with the traditional voices of his *auctores*, the poet constantly encounters the dissonance of those voices'. In the parliament, Chaucer shows the same fragmentation and multiplicity in society as he sensed in himself. The parliament shows a 'breakdown of order and communication produced by the very existence of differing individual styles'. The parliament itself fragments in the same way as the whole poem, showing nature dissolving into flux under the drives and desires of individuals. The poem is finally 're-authorized' by a return to an authorised model which highlights its personal and subjective limitations. A world view is affirmed at the expense of the individual views, but there is no confidence in the unity and harmony of the end. Culture is sustained in traditional forms only if all are self-limiting. Robert Jordan (1987) also finds the ending 'collapsing levels of illusion and homogenizing absolutely differentiated states of being'. But the point is not in this artificial compaction but in the inclusive display of styles, tone and aspects of love. The great virtue of the poem is accommodation; it 'subordinates narrative continuity to a mode of presentation that is expository and spatial rather than developmental and temporal...[it is] a poem without a center and without a denouement'.

Traditional form and creative innovation

It was recognised early that *PF* follows the form of the French love-visions, and Derek Brewer (1958) shows that it is the first poem to combine love-vision and the *demande d'amour* forms. Other critics have focused on one or other element of the composite form, but find in any case subversion, parody or playfulness characterising Chaucer's usage. Thomas Reed (1980) sees Chaucer frustrating and overturning the expectations of literary debate, submerging the original opposition in the greater question the poem asks of whether to pursue or eschew physical love. The form, which seems to demand choice and resolution, is used here to say that no choice need be made and multiplicity can be accepted; Nature accommodates all views and none is rejected immediately.

Charles Owen (1953) sees Chaucer combining realism and convention to parody the form of dream-poetry, showing his amused understanding of the form before abandoning it. Constance Hieatt (1967) notes that Chaucer uses the conventions of the courtly love-vision to undercut the courtly love sentiment, but also detects patterns of real dreams linking the apparently disparate parts. James Winny (1973) finds comedy and realism undermining the poem; as realism creeps in, the dream 'wears thin', common sense threatens to undermine the courtly tradition and *fin amour*. For Gardiner Stillwell (1950), though, the comedy which emerges from incongruities, irony, contrasts and partial views of love is the unifying principle. He sees Chaucer playing with literary forms, finally producing a 'comedy of medieval manners and ideas adapted to the framework of the love-vision'. Boitani (1986) also sees Chaucer playing with our expectations of form, as the poem moves both towards and away from the promised material. The summary of Scipio's dream frustrates our expectations, the dreamer's tour around the park and temple move back towards it, the parliament moves away from it again, but finally the *demande d'amour* returns to the anticipated point.

Others have looked not simply at *PF*'s relation to its models but to its sources. The most comprehensive study of this type is Bennett (1957) who gives a sequential reading of the poem, identifying the sources of Chaucer's borrowings and allusions. It combines New Critical close reading with an account of the effects Chaucer's alterations to his source material achieve. For example, in the description of the park and temple, Chaucer's changes to his sources make the scene increasingly sinister, complex and ambiguous while retaining elements of realism. Combining the neoplatonic principle of plenitude, the Garden of Eden and the garden landscape familiar from Le Roman de la Rose, Chaucer is being innovative.

Larry Sklute (1981) finds a rather different response to the literary heritage. He sees Chaucer rejecting Alain de Lille's neoplatonism and the theory of perfection in diversity (the 'principle of plenitude'). In his reading, Nature is dominated by predators and tyrants, self-seeking views of common profit, and the 'fierce, unreflexive egotism' of the three eagles. Reason is partial and restricted, and Nature is as ready to accept one kind of 'reason' as any other, since there is no absolute answer to the dispute. The final song is a specific celebration for this particular group, and is not an authoritative image of harmony.

As we have seen, H.M. Leicester (1974) discerned Chaucer responding to the multiplicity of his rhetorical and literary heritage, which he took as a challenge to his ability to select and unite elements. The stylisation of the various portions of the poem links them to authorities but isolates them as 'rhetorical blocks which are conspicuously disjunct from one another in style, meaning and implications'. The disjunction directs us to the rhetorical function of the materials. The poem displays an enjoyment of imitation of literary tradition for its own sake, but Chaucer also varies traditional models to communicate a personal, non-traditional message. The original 'project' of the poem is deliberately thwarted as Chaucer focuses on the reduced social issue of the bird debate which creates a 'generalized social image which is a correlative of the psychological situation he presented earlier'. Chaucer explores individualism before retracting and 'reauthorising'.

Larry Sklute's view that the poem rejects authority and asserts the value of individual opinion is shared by David Aers (1981). He shows Scipio's dream presented as dogmatic, nationalistic and limited because it is subjective and does not question the nature of common profit. The poem thus challenges the timeless and objective nature of authority, which tends to turn exploratory concepts into dogma. The dreamer rejects such exclusive interpretation of his own dream which has multiple viewpoints and no moral boundaries, making dogmatic assertion impossible. He continues to read in an inevitably open-ended search 'resistant to authoritative and dogmatic closures of all kinds'. Having undermined authority, Chaucer moves away from using it, both in *PF* and in other works, towards presenting multiple views and voices, most obviously in *CT*.

The House of Fame

If the connections between the parts of the *PF* have proved troublesome, the disjunctions of *HF* are still worse. On a first reading, it can seem puzzling, even meaningless: a poem that falls apart at the seams. It introduces itself as a love-vision, borrows the form of love-vision, and then becomes preoccupied with poetic creativity and the arbitrary nature of Fame. What happens to love?

The poem's first notable critic, W.O. Sypherd (1907, 1915), recognised that it is well balanced, but other early critics sometimes condemned the poem as a half-baked collection of unrelated episodes, unbalanced and in a jarring variety of tones. Even critics who should know better have been inclined to dismiss the poem as unartistic. Thus Charles Muscatine (1957) says it is 'most charitably seen as an experiment, wherein the poet's energy and imagination by far outrun his sense of form' and in which the eagle's lecture 'has no describable function beyond its intrinsic humour'. The conjunction of different styles he finds 'violent'. Robert Burlin (1977) says it contains 'some of the flattest stretches [Chaucer] ever wrote', and Larry Sklute (1984) finds the poem 'at best inconclusive, at worst incoherent'.

Some critics have tried to force the elements into conformity, finding that both Venus' traditional connection with literary creation and the emphasis on rumour in the story of Dido link the themes of love, fame and poetic art. Paul Ruggiers (1953) argues for a 'universalizing impulse' which increases the scope of the poem from love to Fame, which includes love. Derek Traversi (1987) has the dreamer learn that poetic authority (the product of Fame) does not accurately depict the confusing and conflicting elements of love, and that his own poetic work must accommodate and reflect the disorder of life seen in the House of Rumour. But others draw various conclusions from a perception that the elements of the poem, including the themes of love and fame, are not integrated. For Alfred David (1960), the poem moves progressively further away from the ostensible goal of love. The point of the poem is literary satire, its 'central structural idea' being the comic disillusionment of the expectations and aspirations of the dreamer. Because the dreamer is an ignorant imitator of courtly style, the poem's content and ignoble characters undercut its high style. Robert Burlin (1977) suspects that its 'rambling "gothic" parataxis' betrays Chaucer's lack of interest in and uncertainty about what he was doing in a poem which may have been a commissioned work. On the other hand, Boitani (1982) finds the poem deliberately offering a 'series of allusions and hints' rather than a coherent unity, and Robert Jordan (1987) sees the different styles and sections as a deliberate attempt to produce a collage whose point is diversity and in which the only unity is the narrative act that joins the parts together.

Again some have felt that a historical occasion might be the missing link which would have given the poem cohesion. But the poem is not particularly occasional: its events are bizarre and abstruse, and the only fixing point for an occasion is the missing speech of the man of great authority at the end. For a while attention, therefore, focused not on what the poem said, but on what the poem might have said had it continued. This is surely an odd way to approach any work, but the unwritten ending of *HF* has remained a focal point even in more sophisticated treatments.

The silence of the 'man of great authority' and the voice of the poet
The earliest critics supposed the poem may have introduced some court gossip, news or slander, or perhaps a collection of stories similar to *CT*. Others have since suggested that the man of authority could be an 'auctor' who would make some pronouncement on poetry or love. Thus Donald Baker (1960) proposes Virgil delivering a justification of poetry, Paul Ruggiers (1953) suggests Boethius denouncing earthly mutability, and R.C. Goffin (1943) suggests Boccaccio. Kay Stevenson (1978) gives a guide to the postulated endings dividing them into three types: specific tidings (making the poem occasional), entertainments or stories (making *HF* a prologue) and an incisive analysis of themes delivered by a

figure of authority. The last she finds least likely and least Chaucerian, since it would give the poem an explicit resolution which would spoil its balanced and contrasting elements. Either of the other types would undercut or limit the poem. Stevenson concludes that the poem is best unended. (Kittredge had earlier been grateful for the lack of an end as it allowed him free rein to conjecture at will as to how it would have ended.) Donald Fry (1979) finds its unfinished state deliberate and that it 'demonstrates metaphorically the unreliability of transmitting secular knowledge by satirizing the "man of great authority"'. The man of authority's words would be distorted in transmission, so 'the figure is ironic; there is no authority, much less great authority, possible in human secular affairs'.

It is generally agreed that relatively little of the poem is missing, as Sypherd (1915) suggested. His further argument that the poem is neither historical, autobiographical nor intended to introduce a sequence of tales is also commonly accepted. However, his claim that it simply records a marvellous journey given in exchange for the poet's hard work is untenable: we are unlikely to be satisfied with the interpretation that Chaucer's poem is simply a jolly story about a dream in which a loquacious eagle takes a fat poet on a tourist trip with an allegorical itinerary. The question of what *HF* is *about* persists.

Literature, language and the creative imagination
Most scholars now agree that the poem has, in the words of Robert Allen (1956), 'a sustained interest in the nature of literary art', a 'concern with the literary imagination and its relation to the material on which it draws'. But there is still plenty of scope for diverging opinion, and in the past the central issue has not been so readily recognised. Allen pinpoints episodes which demonstrate an interest in literary art, and these have been the focus of attention for later critics, too. In Book I, the retelling of Dido's story shows the creative imagination turning engraved pictures into reported speech. In Book II, the factual knowledge of the eagle is contrasted with the creative and imaginative interests of his passenger, and in the final book Chaucer shows artists and poets modelling exaggerated rumours into poetry which preserves history and tales, making them famous. The conflicting authorities of Virgil and

Ovid telling Dido's story, and the presence of poets in Fame's house, have attracted perennial interest.

Allen's work stresses the poet's relation to his sources and tradition, but the poet uses both literary tradition and private imagination. Chaucer's reception of and thought about texts takes him to the very root of poetic composition, the meaning of language and its relation to the materials – stories, experience, reality – with which poetry deals. We shall look first at Chaucer's appropriation of borrowed materials, but will be quickly returned to his interest in imagination and poetic creativity.

The poem's link with the French dream-poetry tradition has long been recognised, though its relation to the French love-visions is fairly remote. Source study has been dominated instead by its relation to other works, particularly the Italian poets, medieval Latin writers, Ovid, and Virgil. The most comprehensive and detailed study of the poem's relation to its sources is Jack Bennett (1968). Like his book on *PF* (1957), this charts Chaucer's borrowings, allusions and echoes of other texts, giving special prominence to Dante, Virgil and Ovid. Bennett finds Chaucer looking for new material for his poetry, and perhaps finding it in the human experience which forms the substance of rumours. Bennett (1968) is a laborious read and, while the scholarship is admirable and valuable, constructive argument is thin. More readable and coherent are those studies which attempt to explicate relations to individual sources or aspects of the poem's ancestry. David Wallace (1985) compares *HF* with English verse romances, Brunetto Latini's *Tesoretto* and Boccaccio's *Amorosa Visione*, following a line similar to that of Patricia Kean (1972) in demonstrating that the poem 'measures the distance between the practice of English making and the prospect of English poetry' as Chaucer, like Boccaccio, struggles to find a vernacular poetic voice. B.G. Koonce (1966) concentrates on elements borrowed from Dante. Sheila Delany (1968) argues that the 14th-century *Ovid Moralisé* influenced Chaucer's depiction of fame and suggested the interest in conflicting literary authorities. F.M. Fyler (1979) relates Chaucer's process to Ovid's techniques, finding 'Chaucer's primary, unifying purpose, like Ovid's, is to explore the limits of human understanding' and Chaucer 'rephrases Ovid's central awareness of human limitations...using the Ovidian trick of building structures that immediately fall apart'. Joseph Grennen

(1984) suggests that Plato's *Timaeus* and Calcidius' commentary on it together provide an important source, as Chaucer parodies the philosophical quest and celestial vision, and produces a playful study of Plato's epistemological problems.

A more sharply focused full-length study than Bennett (1968) is Piero Boitani's exploration (1984) of the literary and cultural background of Chaucer's depiction of the figure of Fame. The first two thirds of his book are devoted to an analysis of the representation of Fame in Classical, Hebraic and medieval European tradition (particularly in Dante, Boccaccio and Petrarch). Boitani collects attitudes, philosophies and images commonly associated with Fame and explains the etymological connections between different aspects and categories of fame. The last part of the book traces Chaucer's selection, use and rejection of traditional elements. Chaucer is, Boitani says, aware of remoulding traditional knowledge and culture into fiction in a poem which represents 'the first, if timid and partly ironical, exploration of archetypal imagery in English literature, the first poem that goes back to the very roots of our imagination'. Chaucer chooses images and traditions with multiple meanings, adding to the scope of his poem by alluding to elements he does not use explicitly. He holds different ideas and images open at the same time, without committing himself to following any one tradition but accepting the whole as 'the necessary components of his image of poetry'. His object is to show the diversity of literary tradition, heritage and culture, depicting in Fame's house 'the image of himself that Western man has consecrated and transmitted in his entire literary tradition'.

It is this collision of different styles, which Muscatine finds 'violent', that Patricia Kean (1972) considers most inspiring in the poem. She finds *HF* a treasure-house of pillaged styles and voices from European and English literary tradition successfully integrated into the eagle's 'unmistakably English accent'. She gives a detailed close reading of the textural and tonal range of the poem and its choppy juxtapositions of elements from different traditions, finding the verse 'bending, stretching, as it were elasticizing...the English poetic language'. For her, this gets very close to the main theme of the poem which she describes as the 'relation of poetry to the traditions which form its material'.

Boitani (1984) interprets Chaucer's treatment of language rather differently, seeing in it an investigation of the poet's raw material that goes beyond the 'roots of the imagination' to the very nature of words themselves. The House of Rumour extends the scope of the investigation to show the transformation of event into narrative account, of deed into word. It is here that 'reality [is] fragmented and transformed into its narrative sign'. It is the last part of Boitani's book which is the most interesting. Here the eagle's definition of sound as 'broken air' is seen as introducing the issue which is developed in the House of Rumour – the relation of a word to what it signifies. The sounds which fly from the House of Rumour are given a meaning at Fame's castle where the 'official' tellers and their literary heritage impose a meaning on the raw sound. Fiction is then a blend of true and false, acts turned into words which are moulded by tradition but which are, at the same time, only broken air, a sign which both is and is not arbitrary. Boitani introduces this approach late in the book, though HF is clearly a poem which could support an extended and rigorous deconstructionist reading.

Authority and experience: the epistemological equation

Literary tradition embodied in the words of 'auctorite', is only one source of knowledge and poetic material; just as important is experience. The familiar Chaucerian dichotomy of authority and experience is, in HF, worked out as experience is moulded into authority.

F.M. Fyler (1979) sees HF polarising experience and authority as sources for the poet. The proem shows experience defying classification as the narrator struggles with dream theory. The first book shows the conflict between the two authorities for the Dido story, and the narrator's subjective involvement as he retells it. The second book demonstrates fragmentary and practical knowledge that is no better than authority: although it is clear in trivial matters, it is 'as confusing as dreams and books in essentials'. The last book consolidates the message, revisiting authority in Fame's palace and experience in the House of Rumour. For Boitani (1982), this pattern shows the 'matter' of poetry expanding from the (authority) categories in the temple of Venus to include everday experience in the House of Rumour.

Some critics concentrate on either authority or experience. Sheila Delany (1972) focuses on authority in exploring Chaucer's problem with the different claims of diverse literary traditions. The poem is not incoherent but is necessarily incongruous because 'incongruity is its subject, is the essence of fame'. Delany discusses several moments of the poem in detail, uncovering the traditions which lie behind them and inform their meaning. Thus the story of Dido and Aeneas uses two conflicting sources to show the unreliability of fame and demonstrate the poet's problem with tradition. Amongst the meanings of the word 'phantom' she finds one which would be most potent for Chaucer, the 'deception of the written word'. The iconography of Fame's palace shows conflicting literary accounts of events as history in the past becomes known in or hidden from the present. The House of Rumour presents the other part of the process, with the present experience becoming history. The House of Rumour shows the real material of poetry, daily life, but this is not a useful substitute for authority and tradition since it too is unreliable. The poem demonstrates Chaucer's sceptical view of authority and empiricism and replaces them with a declaration of faith. Delany concludes that the poem is ultimately unfinishable: its contradiction (as a 'literary statement about the unreliability of literary statements') cannot be resolved in the terms it has set up. Robert Burlin (1977) agrees in large part with Delany, but finds Chaucer here 'less fideistic than skeptical'. The poem parodies the dream-vision form and denies the distinction between authority and experience, which are both 'facets of a unified way of knowing through the imagination'. Further, 'the parodic dissolution of the epistemological antithesis verges on yet another indirect apology for the poetic imagination'.

Experience presupposes personal engagement, and the narrator's character or involvement becomes more of an issue for critics who concentrate on this element. Larry Sklute (1984) finds the inconclusiveness of the poem emerging from the 'strange interaction of the persona and his experience'. Book I presents anxiety about the poet's control of his material and his ability as a poet. Book II describes the relationship between the poet and his medium. But the teller is intrusive, interpolating his own response to the material when he tells the tale of Dido and Aeneas rather than narrating the authoritative events to elicit our response. Sklute argues that although the poem seems to move towards meaning it becomes insubstantial, failing to answer the issues it raises, and to give the explanation both we and the dreamer expect.

James Winny (1973) sees this frustration as inevitable. The man of great authority must be related in some way to the production of poetry, so the 'inner significance of [Chaucer's] metaphor was about to disclose itself' when he must reveal the 'nature and behaviour of the creative consciousness'. However, for Beryl Rowland (1981) this is precisely what the poem does do. She relates the creative process depicted in the poem to contemporary treatises on memory, showing the poet's art following the same principles as the lessons in memory, which encourage the student to visualise an image for each item and then recall the sequence in order. The poet also takes words and transforms them into pictures, then finally recalls the images in order. In *HF* words appear before Fame in the visual image of the person that spoke them. Chaucer 'fully exposes the mental structures to his audience, externalizing the memory process to show how memory creates a poem'.

Robert Jordan (1987) agrees that the poem is about the creative process, but its intention is to display the act of writing. For this reason the 'surface' intrudes on our reading, keeping a glittering garment of rhetoric and stylistic diversity before our eyes to 'accentuate [Chaucer's] controlling presence'. However, what we see in the protagonist is a 'writer (or teller) out of control – appealing for help, digressing shamelessly, worrying about his accuracy'. By contrast, Donald Fry (1979) sees Chaucer distrusting authorities and the 'distortion of transmitted know-ledge' and trusting only his own art.

Fetheres of philosophye

Few would deny that there are elements of Boethian philosophy in *HF*. The arbitrariness of Fame's judgments promotes the Boethian shunning of earthly vanities. But Boethian readings can be discordantly sombre. Charles Tisdale (1973) sees a link between the influences of Virgil and Boethius. For him, Aeneas is a model of medieval man wandering in his life journey and tempted by carnality. This is similar to the narrator's situation and, like Aeneas recalled by Mercury, the narrator is finally drawn back to the right path, in this case through the agency of the eagle. The poem thus fuses Virgilian reason and Boethian wisdom, and perhaps reflects a significant event in Chaucer's own life. However, this view ignores the Ovidian sympathy for and centrality of Dido in *HF*: the story is really hers, not a tale of Aeneas' salvation from the sins of the flesh.

B.G. Koonce (1966) takes a similar approach, elaborating the vanity of worldly fame in an exegetical reading that traces the development of the poem's elements and finds Christian charity at its heart. Koonce divides fame into two, earthly and heavenly. It is of course sinful to seek earthly fame, and Boethius links it with false good. Again, Aeneas is an exiled pilgrim imaging the soul's pilgrimage to its true home. The desert is the land of carnal love, and the temple of Venus is an inversion of the temple of Christ, signifying the absence of God in the idolatrous heart. The eagle which saves the dreamer from this desert is an agent of Christ and of 'the intellect infused with Grace, turning to God with devotion'. The flight with the eagle purges the dreamer, enabling him to look down without fear and see the true nature of the world. Fame's palace is a pastiche of a church, and an inversion of the destination of true fame. Through the guidance of the eagle (reason) the dreamer is shown in the houses of Fame and Rumour the nature of false fame, the vanity of trusting Fame's judgments, and the reality of the world. He has 'penetrated the maze of human error and observed the source of the distorted tidings which make up [Fame's] fickle decrees'. Koonce concludes that the message of the man of great authority would be a message of salvation and suggests that the poem may have been intended for a Christmas or Advent celebration.

Sheila Delany (1972) puts a different emphasis on Christian faith, finding in the narrator's faith a means of circumventing the epistemological questions of authority and Aristotelian empiricism that the poem raises. Chaucer several times challenges traditional authority on serious topics. The dreamer is sceptical of the eagle's empirical, scientific and Aristotelean beliefs, as they conflict with Christian doctrine, and he makes a statement of faith which denies the need for empirical knowledge. But though the narrator's problem at first seemed to be choice (between authorities, traditions, types of knowledge etc.) he finally learns that he does not need to choose. Faith obviates the need to choose, and 'if the Narrator is committed to anything he is committed to pluralism'.

The Legend of Good Women

One question has dominated the rather scant criticism of *LGW*: is the poem any good? A second question is almost a rephrasing of this: is it intended seriously or ironically? It has seemed to most critics that if the poem is intended seriously it is bad; only deliberate irony could account for the tedious tales poorly told with an odd emphasis on inconsequential or irrelevant details.

Bad poetry in good faith?

The most frequently discussed part of *LGW* has been the dream prologue, partly because critics have found this the most satisfactory section. It is charming and humorous and presents a narrator who has written Chaucer's poems – dare we say he is Chaucer? The only difficulty is that there are two versions of the Prologue, once called A and B and now designated G and F respectively after manuscripts preserving the two versions, Cambridge University Gg. IV. 27 and Fairfax 16. G is probably the later, but Donald Rowe (1988) has recently denied that their order can be determined, and suggests that Chaucer intended the two to co-exist, catering for different audiences.

The trouble really starts when we turn the page and read the legends. Starting with the legend of Cleopatra (hardly renowned for her saintly virtue), the narrator (or Chaucer) fudges the issue. Cleopatra's tale dwells on irrelevancies, dismisses her political role, makes claims for her that her history does not support, and treats her suicide (committed with 'good cheer') reductively. This sets the tone for the remainder. The good women's goodness resides largely in suffering and death; where they are truly great, they are reduced by the narrator; their lives are inappropriately moulded to the demands of the legendary form, and a goodly part of the tales are given over to men, and their political and social dealings. A few critics have tried to defend the legends as straight and sincerely-intended narratives, but the dominant opinions have been either that *LGW* is simply bad or that it is ironic and the tales are badly told for a reason.

The debate over whether *LGW* is satirically intended began with a vituperative sequence of articles by H.C. Goddard and John Livingstone Lowes in 1908 and 1909. Lowes maintained that Chaucer 'accepted [the women] at their conventional appraisal' and intended no satire. Goddard claimed that the poem satirised women, and was perhaps making fun at the expense of a royal request. That the legends are tedious and not life-like is apparently part of the joke. In penance for the act Chaucer has not committed, but of which the God of Love accuses him, Chaucer commits the crime of slandering women. Lowes responded, refuting Goddard's argument step by step and quoting it so extensively it is hardly worth reading Goddard's article separately.

If Chaucer is being satirical, he may be satirising women (in an anti-feminist poem) or satirising the courtly tradition, or the perceived chauvinism of the God of Love, or men (in a pro-feminist poem). John McCall (1979) argues that it is 'perverse' to find the women satirised as Goddard suggests: men are the objects of satire and irony, with the 'good' men and heroes being upstaged and the others depicted as 'cowardly villains'. The work praises the love and hope shown by the women, Cupid represents good, natural love, and the poem is an appropriate seasonal celebration honouring honest love.

It is revealing (even 'perverse'), that McCall finds a legend of good *women* focusing on men. Most readers consider the women to be central, even if they are not all 'good' in our estimation. Elaine Tuttle Hansen (1983) defends the position and integrity of the women, finding the satire directed against Cupid and the narrator, and the anti-feminist tradition to which they subscribe. However, the prominence of men is suggested within the poem: the narrator expresses particularly male interests – in giving extended treatment to the sea battle in Cleopatra's legend, for example – and finds the women boring. Hansen suggests that the narrator may not share Cupid's anti-feminism, but botches the penance to ridicule and undermine his code. Robert Frank (1972) finds the courtly love tradition parodied in the God of Love and in the narrator's ridiculous worship of the daisy without intending praise of a real woman. Edmund Reiss (1976) also sees the poem pointing out the inadequacies of the literary tradition of love. He identifies the phrase 'fyn loyynge' as relating to ideal love, linked with religion and with marital love. The God of Love and Alceste undercut the ideal, as do many of the legends, but it 'remains to make us aware of the various inadequacies of love' detailed in the poem.

Donald Rowe (1988) turns the question of ironic intent on its head. He sees *LGW* dramatising its own writing: the poet's poem (*LGW*) undercuts and makes ironic the narrator's poem (the legends). The issue of irony then comes from within the poem itself, as the poet presents ironically the narrator's (unironic) struggle with his material. The dilemma of how to relate the Ovidian narratives to the demand of Alceste is the narrator's problem which we observe. Through the gap between the narrator and Chaucer, the poet also depicts the cultural and individual restrictions on perception, exposes the futility of trying to mould art to fashion or personal desire, and the difficulty of determining and re-expressing truths from old books – or indeed, any truth – within the limits of language.

Incomplete, inconclusive or unfinished?

It appears that *LGW* is unfinished. It does not fulfil the plan described in the Prologue, nor give the 25 legends (or 15) referred to by Chaucer elsewhere, and the last legend (of Hypermnestra) has seemed incomplete to many readers. It was traditionally assumed that Chaucer became bored with the task (indeed he says he is 'agroted' with it) and perhaps left it unfinished because he too was overcome by the tedium of the not-very-good women. This has been linked with the theory that *LGW* was commissioned, probably by or for Queen Anne, and that Chaucer was less than enthusiastic about the project from the start. Robert Max Garrett (1923) suspected Chaucer found the task distasteful and approached it with derision; Larry Sklute (1984) thinks the stories were tedious because the work really was imposed as a penance of some kind, and Robert Jordan (1987) considers the work a 'minor occasional piece' restricted by the demands of its occasion. Robert Burlin (1977) (who, it must be admitted, thinks the poem a 'colossal blunder') is alone in finding a more positive trace of the occasion: 'the demands of an occasion as much as the choice of a fashionable genre help to account for the implicit speculation on the nature and validity of the poetic process'.

Robert Frank (1972) defends *LGW* against claims that Chaucer was bored with it, citing three types of evidence: firstly, most lines which suggest Chaucer's boredom are simply rhetorical devices to compact the stories; secondly, the narrator's tone mixes humour and seriousness and we should not take all he says at face value; and thirdly, Chaucer left many works unfinished, but we do not assume he was bored with the others, so why make this assumption about *LGW*? Frank (1975) does not deny that it is unfinished, and later suggests that far from boring Chaucer, *LGW* inspired him to attempt a more ambitious work in the same form, *CT*. N.F. Blake (1984) thinks the common belief that Chaucer left many works unfinished is hasty and simplistic, and argues that part of *LGW* and other works may have been lost in transmission. Larry Sklute (1984) agrees that *LGW* is unfinished, but thinks that this is not the important issue; he finds it conclusive in its plan 'to reiterate by different examples a continuously singular theme'. The conclusiveness of this 'outer form' is established as soon as the series of legends is under way.

An argument of a different kind suggests that *LGW* is as complete as Chaucer intended it to be. Donald Rowe's sophisticated reading (1988) of the poem as a double-layer fiction in which the poet shows himself writing it, finds *LGW*'s incompleteness does not preclude its being finished. Because Alceste demanded that the narrator spend all his life writing the legends, they must have an arbitrary end when he dies. Further, Alceste declares that all lovers are false, so the narrator-lover must also be false and give up before he finishes. Rowe supports his case by citing elements of closure in the structure and motifs of *LGW* that show the poem is closed, although the sequence is not (and cannot be) complete.

Love and literature
While the themes of love and literature seem antagonistic in *HF*, in *LGW* they are happily coupled. In the first book-length study of *LGW*, Robert Worth Frank (1972) argues that the legends should be taken as effective narratives which are moving in their own right and which exploit our natural interest in story as patterned and meaningful experience. The poem is, he says, about the proper material of poetry. By parodying courtly tradition and the form of moralised pagan legend, Chaucer shows that a wider body of material is suitable for poetic treatment. Lisa Kiser (1983), too, sees in *LGW* Chaucer's manifesto for the right matter of poetry. Alceste 'embodies Chaucer's principle of uniting Classical and Christian traditions' and exemplifies his principle of translation, preserving Classical truth in his own poetry.

Not only the matter of poetry, but its form is at issue. The Classical legends appropriated to demonstrate a tenet of the courtly tradition of love embody a disparity between form and subject. The unsuitability of many of the women as paragons of exemplary goodness has been frequently noted. The impression is of women's histories uncomfortably forced into unsuitable moulds. John Fyler (1979) considers that the details of the stories 'resist [the narrator's] efforts to prod them into a hagiographical mold'. The narrator cuts anything which reveals the bad side of the women and denies their will and nobility by removing the context of their actions. (For example, by making no reference to Hypermnestra's 49 sisters who did murder their husbands, he removes the uniqueness of her virtue.) Similarly, he tries to fit the men, even Pyramus, into a standard role of evil-doers. Hansen (1983) notes this, too, pointing out that the few good men die for love, like the women. Fyler sees the poem attempting a narrow focus by enforcing a polarisation and supporting one side against the other.

If the women's lives do not fit the pattern of moralised legend endorsing love, this may be because the narrator is unskilled, or because he (or Chaucer) is rebelling against the plan of Alceste and the God of Love. It is commonly recognised that the God of Love's criticism of Chaucer's works shows he has misunderstood them; he is, in Fyler's words, 'a rather literal-minded reader'. Alceste's defence is little better: she acknowledges such inadequacies that the poet might prefer the God's charges. Kiser sees the God of Love's failure as his attempt to read Chaucer's poetry as exempla. Alceste recognises his error and defends the poet using a variety of techniques which hide the truth of the matter – that Chaucer did freely write poems which offend against the decorum of courtly love. Alceste humorously sets up the penance which involves Chaucer writing the type of story the God of Love thinks he has already written: limited, moralistic and didactic. In Kiser's view, the mismatch between matter and form is intended to undermine the God of Love's plan. Chaucer demonstrates his rejection of the God's narrow view of stories by making the legends unsatisfactory, betraying the women (and the good men) as he adapts their tales to the unsuitable shape demanded. The result shows that the God of Love's way of reading literature is untenable:

it violates the character of the sources and abuses the Classical tradition.

This concern with literary form imposed on resistant experience recalls the process of making literature examined in *HF*. The dual claims of authority and experience to provide and shape the poet's material surface again in the Prologue to *LGW*. Robert Payne (1963) finds in the Prologue a swing between authority and experience as the narrator goes from books to enjoying the spring and then back to his books in search of legends. The implication is that 'tradition preserves at the level of generalized (universal) applicability the meanings or values of the facts of experience'. Art involves a reconciliation through language of tradition, practical experience and ideal knowledge, often given in the form of dreams or visions. The familiar movement from book to dream to new book is repeated in essence, but the specific book is now replaced by the traditional literary inheritance that furnishes the legends. For Robert Burlin (1977), the dream is parodic, but brings together experience and authority, polarised in the waking section, to show them to be 'interpenetrating and inseparable'. On the other hand, Goddard (1909) finds the poem a 'powerful protest against the domination of authority, a defense of experience as the only ultimately valid basis for knowledge'.

From the poet's materials of literary authority and experience it is a short step to the art of poetry itself. In the Prologue, Payne (1975) sees Chaucer remaking his image of himself as a poet in search of knowledge, authority and poetic art. In it 'the poet's pursuit...of a knowledge of love...evolves into a kind of symbolic definition of the perplexities and limitations of knowledge, love and art as they had been experienced by the poet of the [dream-poems] and *Troilus and Criseyde*'. While the narrator is reconstructed from his figure in Chaucer's earlier works, Alceste is reconstructed from the works of others, and 'what he confronts in Alceste is not very different from what he confronts in himself'. This final statement of Payne's is transformed into a whole reading of the poem by Lisa Kiser, who describes it as an exploration of the poetic art in which Alceste is a symbol of Chaucer's poetic creativity. The daisy/Alceste mediates the bright light of the truth (the sun) reflecting and imitating it. The daisy demonstrates the proper use of metaphor – a brief life dedicated to communicating the truth lucidly.

The suggestion that the poet reveals important spiritual truth through telling his classical tales is presented as a more extravagant claim by Rowe (1988). He argues that Chaucer shows in the sequence of legends a descent into hell and partial ascent back out again, through which the reader may be brought to enlightenment. The pattern of legends – two telling of faithful love, two of betrayal, two of tyranny and then two more of betrayal, signalling re-emergence from the abyss – follows that of Dante's voyage in L'Inferno. The aim is the same as Dante's: to arrive at eternal truth through reading the messages of nature (in the Prologue) and classical tales. Stopping short of saying that the narrator is sacrificed for the benefit of the reader, Rowe commends Chaucer's putting himself in danger by meddling with old tales of sin in order to enable the reader to learn a valuable moral lesson.

Chapter 5
'Songes, compleintes, roundels, virelayes' and 'Anelida and Arcite'

Chaucer refers in *LGW* to having written 'balades, roundels, [and] virelayes' and in his *Retraction* to 'many a song and many a leccherous lay'. There remain only envoys, complaints and lyrics; there are no ballads, no roundels outside *PF*, no virelays and, sadly, no lecherous lays.

Chaucer's short poems have attracted little critical attention (and less acclaim) until very recently. They are often grouped together as 'minor' poems, though some are exquisite. Their only common feature is that they are short. This is a poor starting point for literary appreciation, and few critics have dealt meaningfully with the poems collectively. What criticism there is focuses on their sources and on the evidence they afford of Chaucer's early poetic development.

The best study of the short poems as a group is by Patricia Kean (1972). She finds Chaucer developing in them a way of communicating to a sophisticated audience, and sometimes to close friends, in an 'urbane' tone. The poems share jokes and intimacies, using a conversational and colloquial style as if inviting us to overhear and enjoy a private conversation. Those poems which use the mannered terms of love and courtliness restrict their audience to those who share knowledge of the conventions. She suggests that Chaucer adapted Italian poetic forms for an audience familiar with French forms, skilfully combining and moulding the two influences, maybe in response to his audience's interest in new poetry. They perhaps helped create a suitable milieu and prepare a receptive audience for his longer works. Kean finds similarities in tone, vocabulary and intention in the short poems which make her consideration of them together productive. Earle Birney (1939) also relates the short poems to Chaucer's development, this time focussing on his irony. He shows and explicates ironies in the short poems, BD, and some of CT to show that 'Chaucer was always an ironist'.

Other critics have concentrated on the relation of the short poems to French verse. Wolfgang Clemen (1963) sees Chaucer struggling in the early short poems with very artificial and complex French models, sometimes only partially succeeding in adapting them to his requirements and to the English language. But in the later 'Complaint of Mars' and in 'Anelida and Arcite', Chaucer skilfully adapts his sources and models to convey his own interests and concerns. Nancy Dean (1967) detects the influences of Ovid's Heroides in the complaints, Haldeen Braddy (1947) studies the correspondence between Chaucer's poems and those of Graunson, and James Wimsatt (1978) champions the influence of Machaut on Chaucer's works. Braddy does not give rigorous comparative accounts of the suggested sources, but presents the texts for comparison.

Rossell Hope Robbins (1978) postulates a closer link with French tradition, suggesting that Chaucer's earliest poems may have been written in French. His circumstantial evidence includes Chaucerian reference to having written verse in French forms which does not survive. Robbins only describes the types of verse Chaucer may have written, but James Wimsatt produces examples which he considers possibly to be by Chaucer. Chaucer and the Poems of 'Ch' (1982) presents fifteen poems initialled 'Ch' in manuscript, which Wimsatt suggests might be early compositions of Chaucer's, though he concedes that this cannot now be proven.

Of all the lesser poems, the two longer pieces, the 'Complaint of Mars' and 'Anelida and Arcite', have attracted most attention. Criticism of the others is patchy.

'The Complaint of Mars' and the Other Complaints

The most often discussed and most impressive of the complaints is the 'Complaint of Mars'. It was once thought that the 'Complaint of Venus' was a companion piece, but there is no evidence for this, and 'Mars' is now generally treated alone.

John Shirley, a 15th-century scribe, recorded that the 'Complaint of Mars' was written by Chaucer at John of Gaunt's command, and further that 'some men sayne [it] was made by my lady of York doghter to the kyng of Spaygne and my lord of huntyngdon some tyme duc of Exester'. The ensuing search for an allegorically represented historical affair settled on a liaison between John Holland and either Isabel of York or Elizabeth of Lancaster, both daughters of John of Gaunt.

Elizabeth is the favourite candidate and was first proposed by George Cowling in 1926. He dated the action of the poem on astronomical data to 1385, suggesting the work was composed in 1386 as an apology for the marriage of Elizabeth of Lancaster to John Holland, Earl of Huntingdon. Elizabeth had been engaged to the Earl of Pembroke, when she fell in love with Holland, and quickly married him. Alternatively, George Williams (1965) argues that the poem represents the affair between John of Gaunt and Katharine Swynford, Chaucer's wife's sister. He casts William Courtenay, Bishop of London, as Phoebus and Chaucer himself as Mercury. This imaginative reading has John of Gaunt temporarily separated from Katharine, who flees to Chaucer's house for sanctuary. Finding Chaucer out, she hides in the cellar until his return, so the description of Mercury's cave perhaps tells us something about Chaucer's house! He dates the event 12 April 1376, but has no historical evidence to support his theory and there is no record of the two being parted because of scandal. Williams' reading has been deservedly ignored by subsequent critics. Though historical-allegorical readings have generally passed out of fashion now, Nancy Dean (1967) employs the historical significance when she says the poem follows Ovid's pattern in treating an important and heroic moment in a well-known story in a non-heroic fashion.

Cowling's interpretation of the poem was accepted for many years, but his argument has been fiercely attacked recently. In place of the historical view, astrological interpretations and/or detailed textual analysis have become more popular. The most important astrological reading is Chauncey Wood's controversial account of the poem (1970). Rejecting historical readings, he finds the whole poem a condemnation of secular passion and an affirmation of pure Christian love. He draws evidence from the medieval horoscope tradition and the mythographers to support his case that the tale depicts a lecherous union. The conjunction of Mars and Venus in a horoscope presages a lecherous predisposition; the mythographers found in the Ovidian story of Mars and Venus a tale of *virtus* corrupted by *libido* and revealed by truth. All mythographic literary and iconographic treatments of the myth are derisive: none uses it to illustrate virtuous love. John Norton-Smith (1974) rejects Wood's reading as 'entirely wayward'. He too refuses the historical reading, but finds in the poem evidence of interests Chaucer explored further in *Tr*. The poem combines the traditional Classical attributes of Mars and Venus with medieval chivalric and courtly characteristics. He finds all the astrological details significant, and accounts for them fully. The poem shows, he argues, an interest in freewill and determinism, and questions God's purpose in creating love and appetite. Clemen (1963) also notes that the poem illustrates the relationship between free will and determinism in the paradox of a love whose course is determined by spontaneous feeling being represented in the immutable movement of the planets. The poem also raises the question of whether love is by nature constant or variable, both themes revisited in *Tr*. Clemen finds that Mars' complaint moves away from the French models of complaint towards the Latin *planctus* tradition as the poem challenges God's ordering of the world. The poem plays off convention against innovation and the ideal against disillusionment to produce irony.

Irony is tackled further by Edgar S. Laird (1972). He explains that in medieval astronomical terminology the aspect of Venus and Mars is always described as 'privy and secret' 'loving'. The planets in their action described in the poem thus enact and eternally re-enact the myth of Mars and Venus and a model of love as the characters relate to knighthood and 'ladyhood' in a 'complex way'. The action of the poem thus shows betrayal as being amongst the eternal and conventional pains of love.

Chaucer's revitalisation of the French form dominates criticism of the other complaints. Thus Clemen finds Chaucer transforming the purely psychological and abstract concerns of the French complaints into 'images, episodes and dramatic scenes which serve to illustrate [them]'. However, he criticises the 'Complaint Unto Pity' as a completely allegorical piece adopting commonplace allegorical personifications and using conventional language. 'Pity' reflects the movement of the complaint towards formality and convention and away from the immediate expression of feeling, though he acknowledges evidence of Chaucer's later style in the poem in the use of English idiom, to produce 'something like a piece of reasoned prose that at times might actually be "the language of speech"'. In 'A Complaint to His Lady', Chaucer shuns sonorous French terms and aims at 'naive utterance' similar to the 'speaking voice' he developed later. Though unity is sacrified, the conjunctions limit thought in order to show contrast, connections, or to pass to the next idea, and thus Chaucer successfully puts the points of view of both Pity and Cruelty in an effect similar to dialogue.

Charles Nolan (1978/9) finds a more specific combination of styles in the 'Complaint Unto Pity'. He sees it as an attempt, only partially successful, to blend the modes of amorous and legal complaint, using the three-part structure of the legal complaint. The combination intensifies the language, as the effect and nuances of several words which were commonplace in conventional, stylised love lyrics are made fresh and interesting by the legal connotations. The legal content gives weight to the grievance, lending it the force of law, and the presentation of Pity and Cruelty as antagonists at law suggests social as well as personal consequences.

'Anelida and Arcite'

Another complaint, that of Anelida, has also attracted a good deal of attention. Though it is generally assumed that 'Anelida and Arcite' is only a fragment, it has been criticised for its disjointedness and lack of emotional involvement. It is often mentioned in tandem with *KnT* because the name of the hero, Arcite, is common to both, though Anelida's story seems to bear no relation to the Arcite of *KnT*.

A good close reading is given by Stephen Knight (1973) who finds the invocation promises a mixed style, and the poem then continues to present first a very plain style, then a more decorated style and finally a high style in Anelida's complaint. Chaucer achieves only limited success, however, as the plain style deteriorates into banality and he has not mastered the rhyme royal stanza well enough to perfect the high style, and the poem is 'a failure'.

Form is the main issue of debate, both the poem's unfinished state and comparison of Anelida's complaint with the French complaint poems. Clemen (1963) sees 'Anelida' as an experimental piece attempting new modes of expression, feeling towards something later expressed in *KnT*. He finds the introduction unrelated to the story, with the Boccaccian epic setting quickly dropped for the formality of the French complaint form. Chaucer tries to give the complaint form a new specificity by developing it from a love story and increases its immediacy by presenting it as an epistle rather than mediating it through a narrator. The complaint raises the issue of the value of truth and indeed its existence; Chaucer wants us to sympathise, and to share his concern with the issue, creating greater involvement on the reader's part than the French complaint poems generate. Similarly, the alternation of feelings, the elements of monologue and dialogue, offer more space for the development of feeling than the formal French models.

Comparison with French poems is taken further by James Wimsatt (1970), who links 'Anelida' with the *dits amoureux* of Froissart and Machaut. These also juxtapose rather than integrate Classical material with the main action or story, and the expression of sentiment is the chief unifying force in both French and English poems. He suggests that the sources of *BD* influenced the poem, but finds no similarity of diction. Larry Sklute (1984) finds similarities in the design and use of sources in the 'Anelida' and *BD*. He suggests that Chaucer stopped the poem short because the form could not accommodate the different elements he was trying to combine. On the other hand, *KnT* successfully combines epic and lyric complaint because its leisurely pace allows space for the transitions. Even the fragment we have is inconclusive in its form, as it fails to achieve what it ostensibly sets out to achieve.

Guessing the ending has been almost as common a preoccupation of critics of 'Anelida' as of *HF*. Wimsatt guesses that the poem would have been around 700 lines long and have had a happy ending, with Arcite reunited with Anelida (though whether reunion with such a man as Arcite can be considered a happy ending is a moot point). A more extravagant continuation theory is offered by Michael D. Cherniss in 'Anelida and Arcite: Some Conjectures' (1970), a title which warns us of the flights of fancy to come. He suggests that the 'Anelida' is the start of a dream-poem, sharing structural features and a general 'thematic movement' with the other dream-poems. The concentration on the fact of betrayal rather than the narrative sequence which leads to it raises questions of fate, man's nature, Fortune and other

Boethian issues which 'cry out for some sort of visionary experience' for Anelida. Cherniss imagines the story of *KnT* forming the substance of the poem, either in or after Anelida's dream. This he thinks would console Anelida since she prays to Mars who (arguably) causes Arcite's downfall. He concludes, sensibly, that this plan is a very bad idea and would cause Chaucer such problems that this must be why he abandoned the piece.

John Norton-Smith (1974) goes against the critical consensus in arguing that the poem is complete. He rejects the final stanza as inauthentic; it is not found in all the manuscripts and is not in Chaucer's style. He finds a three-part structure similar to that of the complaints of Mars and to Pity which is in no way experimental, and the combination of elements is not inappropriate. Dating it between *Tr* and *LGW*, he says it is most closely related to the Italian, Theban concerns of *Tr* and the ideas of penance, Ovidian complaint and redress of the wrongs done to woman found in *LGW*. The poem mediates between the tragic and declining pagan world of the end of *Tr* and the legendary, ironically Christian world of the *LGW*. He suggests that it represents Chaucer's farewell to the artificiality of French forms. The poem displays a positive attitude towards the function of poetry; in Anelida's complaint we see poetry preserving the experience which would otherwise be lost. Poetry, the poem shows, 'confers a memorable record in terms of causes and effects in the area of human history both public and private'.

Lyrics

According to Rossell Hope Robbins (1979), Chaucer was the only writer of secular lyric in English in the late 14th century, and was the first to use these French forms in English. Of all Chaucer's poems, the dream-visions and lyrics were the first to be imitated. Robbins traces the French forms Chaucer used, showing how he adapted them, giving a quick account of the form and content, sources and historical significance of each of the lyrics. Wimsatt (1978) also considers sources, especially the influence of Machaut. Of the lyrics, only 'An ABC' and 'To Rosemounde' have attracted much attention.

'An ABC' is often considered one of the earliest of Chaucer's poems because of Speght's 1602 comment (of dubious reliability) that it was composed for Blaunche, the wife of John of Gaunt, who died in 1368. Criticism of the poem sometimes leans heavily on the assumption that it is an early piece. The poem is a free translation of a poem by the French poet Deguileville. Clemen (1963) gives a good account of how Chaucer's poem is an improvement on the French original, replacing over-sophisticated and abstract diction with vivid poetry and graphic and familiar images. It is an early example of how Chaucer enriches and extends the powers of English as a poetic language by adopting words from French.

Edmund Reiss (1966) describes 'An ABC' as a series of variations on the merits of the Virgin which 'goes nowhere'. The series demands changes of focal point and the development of a theme, but Chaucer's changes are static, and he too often uses many of the same words to communicate the same idea. Instead of a cohesive whole, the poem should be seen as a sequence of 23 separate poems or prayers, the sum of which reveals something about the Virgin and Christian ideology. Reiss says that the two characters interact in various ways, with Mary like a mother, lover and helper to the narrator at different times. The characters themselves are static, and although the narrator's tone alternates between prayer, praise and lament, he does not get closer to the Virgin during the course of the poem.

Alfred David (1982) reads 'An ABC' alongside *PrT* and pinpoints similarities and differences in the styles. He answers both Clemen and Reiss, dismissing the theory that the poem is early and shows how far it is from a simple translation. He argues that the repetition and lack of direction in the poem are characteristic features of prayer, and says that the poem 'doesn't go anywhere' because prayer never does. The circularity of its closure is common to prayer, dream and romance; the poem constantly circles around the same point, trying to please and surprise by its elegance and refinement. He explains the graphic quality noted by Clemen, describing how the poem expands clichés about the Virgin, making them into vivid pictures. The rhetoric of the poem is modelled on the lover's complaint, using a courtly and sophisticated style. At the same time, the emotion of the piece is heightened by the contrasts of good and evil, innocence and cruelty, the hope of salvation and fear of damnation. Through these contrasts, a dramatic competition is set up between the Virgin and the devil which gives the poem a romantic character. This is recalled in *PrT* as the characters become polarised and transformed into types of the same foes. The courtly style is appropriate to both 'An ABC' and the Prioress, and together they reveal a 'new and fashionable religiosity that combines gentility with emotion, decorousness with enthusiasm'.

'To Rosemounde' is as far from the religiosity of 'An ABC' as possible. Undoubtedly the best of Chaucer's short poems, it has received more attention than most, partly because it is difficult to pin down the tone of such incongruous images as the lover wallowing in love like a fish drenched in sauce. Tone has naturally been the main focus of interest in the poem.

Reiss (1966) attributes the effectiveness of 'To Rosemounde' to the incongruous blend of sound, rhythm and meaning. The sounds of words suggest the ludicrous and therefore playful tone of the poem, but the poem swings between extremes of exaggeration and 'seemly' expressions. The detachment of the narrator here allows an ironic view of the lady, whereas in 'An ABC' this detachment caused pain, fear and frustration. On the other hand, Robbins (1971) denies that there is irony in the poem and follows others in suggesting that it is addressed to a child, most probably the child bride of Richard II, Isabelle of Valois. He argues that the love terms of the poem are conventional and the work is intended as a compliment.

The best and most sophisticated reading of 'To Rosemounde' is by Edward Vasta (1979). Starting from the incompatability of the language and theme, he shows Chaucer using bourgeois language and images in a courtly form which reveal a narrative sequence which ranges through seeing and falling in love with a woman, to making social contact, to imagined sexual involvement with her. But parallel to this progression is another: the speaker becomes self-obsessed, concentrating increasingly on himself; his love changes to self-love in which Rosemounde becomes quite unnecessary since it does not matter whether or not she favours him. In a poem that is more a dramatic monologue than a lyric, the speaker reveals his own character to be comfortable, mediocre, confident and self-sufficient. The Chaucerian persona revealed and satirised here is much the same as that developed in later works. Chaucer further uses the poem to satirise the forms of love poetry and the ideology of love, since the conventions of love contradict each other and emerge as incompatible with medieval aesthetics and morality.

The Boethian Poems and the Epistles

The poems classed as 'Boethian' are those philosophical pieces which reflect interests fostered by the *Consolation of Philosophy*: 'The Former Age', 'Fortune', 'Gentilesse', 'Lak of Stedfastness', and 'Truth'. However, Patricia Kean (1972) finds them reminiscent of Seneca rather than Boethius, seeing in them an undogmatic conversational style intended to stimulate dicussion, inviting a free interchange between poet and audience.

On the whole, these Boethian poems have received little attention, but the 'Former Age' has inspired a couple of interesting readings. John Norton-Smith (1968) sees it as a political allegory and satire in which Chaucer follows Deschamps in using Boethius to satirise contemporary society. As 'former' is only meaningful when compared with a later example, it demands a comparison between the former and contemporary ages. He sees Richard II as Nimrod, with the poem as a direct condemnation of Richard's rule, untempered by any hope of morality or reform. More recently, A.V.C. Schmidt (1976) has given a close reading of the poem, comparing it with its sources (Boethius and Ovid), and arguing that Chaucer is expressing regret and a type of modest aspiration, at once both serious and non-serious, in the same vein as his other poetry.

John Norton-Smith describes Chaucer as 'the first English poet to master the essentials of the Augustan verse epistle'. Only the envoys to Scogan and Bukton qualify as epistles in the real sense, but we may include the 'Words unto Adam' here as they are ostensibly addressed to an individual.

The 'Envoy de Chaucer a Scogan' has received most attention. Norton-Smith (1966) finds in it a combination of urbane, conversational style and syntax, structural indirection (the point of the envoy is not revealed until the end), and borrowings from Horace. He does not tackle the occasion for the poem, or its real meaning, which have long been debated. Kean's observation (1972) that the poem assumes that the audience shares the poet's awareness of events and values identifies the root of the difficulty. The early suggestion by Walter French (1939) that it may be a tactful refusal on Chaucer's part to write a conciliatory poem for Scogan to give to his scorned mistress has recently been rejected, though it gained acceptance for many years. Alfred David (1969) suggests a different historical scenario, with Scogan writing a poem satirising conventional courtly attitudes. Chaucer's poem plays with the serious issues of mutability and the value of poetry without making conclusive pronouncements.

R.T. Lenaghan (1975) has a different problem with the poem. For him, it is its logic – the progression from love to friendship, from game to an earnest request – which is the central difficulty. Lenaghan isolates seven statements the poem makes to show how its focus shifts, and how the end reasserts the jocular tone of the start and recalls the friendship which justifies the poem. He sees the uncertain relationship between the ironic attitudes and the sincere call for a friend in need as reflecting a basic division in attitudes which is not peculiar to Chaucer. He compares it with Deschamps' lyrics which are both respectful and sceptical of the courtly code. The best response is not to seek logic but to consider the nature of the poem's appeal: the genuineness of the geniality and assertion of friendship. The poem is typical of Chaucer in its combination of game and earnest, its genial irony, its use of love conventions while rejecting the role of the lover, and in its difficult or flawed logic.

This book began with Chaucer's longest poem; it is fitting that it should end with his shortest, his 'Words unto Adam'. How much could Chaucer pack into a seven-line poem? Interest has until recently centred on trying to find a historical model for Adam, but an allegorical reading has emerged which attempts to give the poem wider significance by linking Adam-the-scribe's inadequacies with those of the first Adam. Russell Peck (1975) first formulates the idea, at the end of an article on medieval poetics, and R.E. Kaske develops it (1979). Peck gives the following account of how the poem invites expansion into other areas of reference: 'We recall that other Adam Scriveyn, who gave the name to all the creatures and wrote the first chapter of the book in which we are all characters, whose careless act of negligence and rape left us all, through that inborn human propensity for error, to labor and scrape out our living correcting mistakes. Because of his old errors it becomes our job to renew the work "ofte a-daye"'.

'Adam' returns us to the point at which we started, Chaucer's plea 'after my makyng thow wryte more trewe'. With this explicit reference to the transmission of his texts, and the image it calls up of future readers struggling with a poor version of his art, Chaucer acknowledges the importance and contingency of the written word as he did of the spoken word in *HF*. We also see in it Chaucer sending his work forth with care and concern, just as he dispatches *Tr* in 'Go litel boke', an image more hopeful and positive than the 'Retraccioun' that ended *CT*.

Chapter 6
Conclusion

If a pattern emerges from reading a large body of Chaucer criticism together, it is one of increasing diversification. The variety of approaches to Chaucer's poetry is expanding all the time, though we can trace two trends in recent criticism. The first is a movement away from everything realist towards criticism which is acutely aware of the literariness and intertextuality of Chaucer's poetry. Narrow historicism which tries to trace historical events and trends, biographical techniques which find Chaucer's character in his poetry, and the dramatic readings which look for psychological realism in characterisation, have given way to a recognition of the importance of poetics, of Chaucer's concern with poetry and the role of the poet. Voices and tones replace characters, patterns of Chaucer's thought replace inferred details of his life and character, and an awareness of contemporary philosophy, cosmology, theology and other areas of knowledge replaces the attempt to find the Peasants' Revolt or the betrothal of Richard II in the works. The second trend is the exchange of the search for unity and single conclusions for an acknowledgment of contingency, plurality, uncertainty and tension as deliberate and positive aspects of Chaucer's work. Models for his structures range from 'Gothic' through the iconographic 'interlace' to Jordan's 'inorganic', but they are all a far cry from the roadside drama and the love-vision.

It might seem that criticism now focuses on what could appear at first to be the peripheral issues. On our first reading of *Tr*, our experience of the realist novel predisposes us to assess the characters by realist methods, to look at the success or quality of the relationship between the lovers. Only on a closer reading will we recognise the extended treatment of philosophical issues, or the working out of the problematic relationship between a poet and the authority of literary tradition. The dream-poems, in which these issues are closer to the surface (perhaps because the plots of the dream-poems are so insubstantial) are now attracting more (and more favourable) critical attention than ever before. Fashions in

Chaucer's poetry change, as in everything, but it looks as if the pre-eminence that *Tr* has occupied for so long is finally being challenged. The dream-poems and *CT* are commanding more attention, perhaps because they give more insight into Chaucer's methods and are more overtly concerned with the issues which appeal most strongly to us now: with the whole concept of story-telling, with the uncertain nature of language, the shifting meanings of words and the possibilities of poetic structures. The appeal of *Tr* to readers of a realist bent, that led Kittredge to call it the first novel, is the aspect least interesting to those readers who want to formulate, in Derek Brewer's phrase, a Chaucerian poetic. It is perhaps significant of such a shift in fashion that two influential books on poetics, by Fichte in 1980 and Jordan in 1987 discuss the dream-poems and *CT* at length but make no mention at all of *Tr*.

This is not to say that *Tr* will fall into disrepute, but rather that the other poems are enjoying a renaissance of interest because they come closest to issues of current interest. There is still a long way to go in the direction of exploring Chaucer's attitude towards fiction-making, its process, purpose and validity, and of expressing anew his ideas on language – from the physical, meaningless sound to the complexity of cultural and personal resonance. Some of the most exciting and promising of recent criticism points us in these directions, and each student of Chaucer can find a unique path. Several writers (not Chaucerian critics) have pointed out that current philosophical developments, including positivism and semiology and the erosion of confidence in any fixed world view, bring us closer to the intellectual scene in the 14th century than we have been in 600 years. It is hardly surprising then that it is those of Chaucer's poems that deal most overtly with these issues that are again attracting our attention.

From the last couple of paragraphs, it might be inferred that Chaucer criticism is suddenly alive with the activity of post-structuralists. This would seem incongruous, for medievalists generally have a bad press, and are often (with some justification) considered to be at least 20 years behind developments in critical thought. The popular picture of a medievalist is of a dowdy frump in a brown cardigan, shuffling around libraries peering at the curly bits in Latin manuscripts. There are some like this, it is true. But there are others who are bringing deconstructionist, feminist, Marxist, semiotic and other modern approaches to Chaucer, with results which are sometimes fruitful, sometimes provocative and sometimes disappointing. Without getting bogged down in hermeneutics, we must remain sensitive to the danger of bringing to Chaucer's works philosophies and ideas he never dreamt of, and finding in the texts whatever we seek in them. But though Chaucer did not have the vocabulary of modern criticism, his interest in the social role of women, or the contingency of language, is there for us to find and explore in whatever terminology we think fit. All ages have found in Chaucer that which was most appropriate and seemed most apposite to their own times. If Arnold thought Chaucer lacked 'high seriousness' and Lewis thought *Tr* a great celebration of romantic love, we can learn from what we now think of as their mistakes. We can point to the great bulk of lines in *Tr* which do not relate to the story, but to its 'storyness' as evidence of Chaucer's paramount interest in the activity of literature and phenomenon of language, but no doubt the other half of the text, that which does relate the story, lies in wait for those who become too confident: Chaucer wrote a whole poem, not two halves, and his works challenge us to recognise and respect their integrity. I suspect that the modern reader is in many ways less accommodating, less flexible, than the medieval reader, and that we struggle to engage disparate elements meaningfully where the medieval reader could leap ahead to grasp the poem as an entity, enchanting, quirky and profound, stimulating, frustrating and satisfying at the same time. We should not, then, dismiss the work of earlier critics with whom we now disagree. It would be unforgivably arrogant to assume that Kittredge thought *Tr* novelistic because of his own limited perception, for our own perception is no doubt equally limited in other directions. It is valuable instead to investigate why the texts were susceptible to such interpretation; they elicited a response and we should try to understand why. After all, 'Al that is writen is writen for oure doctrine'.

Bibliography

Abbreviations for Journals and Periodicals

Archiv	Archiv für das Studium der neueren Sprachen und Literaturen
CE	College English
ChR	Chaucer Review
Comp Lit	Comparative Literature
ELH	A Journal of English Literary History
JEGP	Journal of English and Germanic Philology
MAe	Medium Aevum
MLN	Modern Language Notes
MP	Modern Philology
NM	Neuphilologische Mitteilungen
PBA	Proceedings of the British Academy
PLL	Papers on Language and Literature
PMLA	Proceedings of the Modern Language Association
PQ	Philological Quarterly
RES	Review of English Studies
RUO	Revue de l'Université d'Ottowa
SAC	Studies in the Age of Chaucer
SE	Studies in English
SP	Studies in Philology

Some Useful Bibliographies

Allen, M. and Fisher, J.H., *The Essential Chaucer* (Mansell Publishing, 1987)

Baird, L.Y., *Bibliography of Chaucer, 1964-1973* (G.K. Hall, 1977)

Baird-Lange, L.Y. and Schnuttgen, H., *A Bibliography of Chaucer 1974-1985* (Archon; D.S. Brewer, 1988)

Crawford, W.R., *Bibliography of Chaucer 1954-1963* (University of Washington Press, 1967)

Griffith, D.D., *Bibliography of Chaucer 1908-1953* (University of Washington Press, 1955)

Hammond, E.P., *Chaucer: A Bibliographical Manual* (Macmillan, 1908; repr. Peter Smith, 1933)

Morris, L.K., *Chaucer Source and Analogue Criticism* (Garland, 1985)

Peck, R.A., *Chaucer's Lyrics and Anelida and Arcite: An Annotated Bibliography 1900-1980* (University of Toronto Press, 1983)

—— *Chaucer Bibliographies: Chaucer's Romaunt of the Rose and Boece, Treatise on the Astrolabe, Equatory of the Planets, Lost Works and Chaucer Apocrypha* (University of Toronto Press, 1988)

Annual Chaucer bibliographies are published in *Studies in the Age of Chaucer* (from 1975/6) and in the *Year's Work in English Studies* (from 1921), and an annual report on research in progress is published in the *Chaucer Review*.

The continuing series of *Chaucer Bibliographies* (University of Toronto Press) and the *Variorum Edition of the Works of Geoffrey Chaucer* (in progress under the general editorship of Paul Ruggiers, University of Oklahoma Press) will provide comprehensive bibliographies on each work.

Bibliography of works cited

Cross-references are marked *.

Aers, D., '*The Parliament of Fowls*: Authority, the Knower and the Known', *ChR* 16 (1981), pp. 1-17

Allen, J.B. and Moritz, T.A., *A Distinction of Stories* (Ohio State University Press, 1981)

Allen, R.J., 'A Recurring Motif in Chaucer's *House of Fame*', *JEGP* 55 (1956), pp. 393-405

Baldwin, R., *The Unity of the Canterbury Tales*, Anglistica 5 (1955)

Baker, D.C., 'Recent Interpretation of Chaucer's *Hous of Fame* and A New Suggestion', *SE* 1 (1960), pp. 97-104

Barney, S. (ed.), *Chaucer's Troilus: Essays in Criticism* (Archon, 1980)

Baum, P.F., 'Chaucer's "Glorious Legende"', *MLN* 60 (1945), pp. 377-81

—— 'Chaucer's Puns', *PMLA* 71 (1956), pp. 225-46 and 'Chaucer's Puns, A Supplemental List', *PMLA* 73 (1958), pp. 167-70

—— *Chaucer's Verse* (Duke University Press, 1961)

Bennett, J.A.W., *The Parlement of Foules: An Interpretation* (Clarendon Press, 1957)

—— *Chaucer's Book of Fame* (Clarendon Press, 1968)

Benson, C.D., *The History of Troy in Middle English Literature* (D.S. Brewer; Rowman and Littlefield, 1980)

—— 'The Canterbury Tales. Personal drama or experiments in poetic variety?' in *Boitani and Mann (1986), pp. 93-108

Benson, L.D., (ed.), *The Learned and the Lewed* (Harvard University Press, 1974)

—— 'The Occasion of *The Parliament of Fowls*', in *The Wisdom of Poetry, Essays in Early English Literature in Honor of Morton W. Bloomfield*, ed. Benson, L.D. and Wenzel, S. (Medieval Institute Publications, Michigan,1982)

—— (ed.), *The Riverside Chaucer* (Houghton Mifflin, 1987)

Bethurum, D., 'Chaucer's Point of View as Narrator in the Love Poems', *PMLA* 74 (1959), pp. 511-20, repr. *Schoek and Taylor, II, pp. 21-31

Birney, E., 'The Beginnings of Chaucer's Irony', *PMLA* 54 (1939), pp. 637-55, repr. *Birney (1985), pp. 54-75

—— 'Chaucer's "Gentil" Manciple and his "Gentil" Tale', *NM* 61 (1960), pp. 257-67, repr. *Birney (1985), pp. 125-33

—— 'Structural Irony within the Summoner's Tale', *Anglia* 78 (1960a), pp. 204-18, repr. *Birney (1985), pp. 109-23

—— *Essays on Chaucerian Irony*, ed. Rowland, B. (Toronto University Press, 1985)

Bishop, I., *Chaucer's Troilus and Criseyde* (University of Bristol, 1981)

Blake, N.F., 'Geoffrey Chaucer, the Critics and the Canon', *Archiv* 221 (1984), pp. 64-79

—— *The Canterbury Tales by Geoffrey Chaucer*: edited from the Hengwrt Manuscript (York Medieval Texts: Edward Arnold, 1980)

Blamires, A., *The Critics Debate: The Canterbury Tales* (Macmillan, 1987)

Bloomfield, M., 'Chaucer's Sense of History', *JEGP* 51 (1952), pp. 301-13, repr. *Bloomfield (1970), pp. 13-26
—— 'Distance and Predestination in *Troilus and Criseyde*', *PMLA* 72 (1957), pp. 14-26, repr. *Schoek and Taylor, II, pp. 196-210
—— 'Authenticating Realism and the Realism of Chaucer', *Thought* 29 (1964), pp. 335-58, repr. *Bloomfield (1970), pp. 175-98
—— *Essays and Explorations* (Harvard University Press, 1970)
Boitani, P., *Chaucer and Boccaccio*, Medium Aevum Monographs 8 (1977)
—— *English Medieval Narrative in the 13th and 14th Centuries*, trans. Hall, J.K. (Cambridge University Press, 1982)
—— *Chaucer and the Imaginary World of Fame* (D.S. Brewer, 1984)
—— 'Old books brought to life in dreams: *The Book of the Duchess, The House of Fame* and *The Parliament of Fowls*', in *Boitani and Mann (1986), pp. 39-57
Boitani, P. and Mann, G., (eds), *The Cambridge Chaucer Companion* (Cambridge University Press, 1986)
Bowden, M., *A Commentary on the General Prologue to the Canterbury Tales* (Macmillan, 1949)
Braddy, H., '*The Parliament of Fowls* in its Relation to Contemporary Events', in Brown, C. (ed.), *Three Chaucer Studies* (Oxford University Press, 1932), II, pp. 7-101
—— *Chaucer and the French Poet Graunson* (Louisiana State University Press, 1947)
Brewer, D.S., 'The Genre of *The Parliament of Fowls*', *MLR* 53 (1958), pp. 321-6, repr. *Brewer (1984), pp. 1-7
—— (ed.), *Geoffrey Chaucer: The Parlement of Foulys* (Manchester University Press, 1960)
—— (ed.), *Chaucer and Chaucerians* (Thomas Nelson and Sons; University of Alabama Press, 1966)
—— 'The Criticism of Chaucer in the Twentieth Century', in *Cawley (1969), pp. 3-28
—— 'Some Metonymic Relationships in Chaucer's Poetry', *Poetica* (1974a), pp. 1-20, repr. *Brewer (1984), pp. 37-53
—— 'Towards a Chaucerian Poetic', *PBA* 60 (1974b), pp. 219-52, repr. *Brewer (1984), pp. 54-79
—— (ed.), *Geoffrey Chaucer, Writers and their Background* (G. Bell and Sons, 1974c)
—— (ed.), *Chaucer: The Critical Heritage*, 2 vols (Routledge and Kegan Paul, 1978)
—— *Chaucer: The Poet as Storyteller* (Macmillan, 1984)
Bronson, B.H., 'The Parlement of Foules Revisited', *ELH* 15 (1948), pp. 247-60
—— '*The Book of the Duchess* Re-opened', *PMLA* 67 (1952), pp.

863-81, repr. *Wagenknecht (1959), pp. 271-94

Bryan, W.F. and Dempster, G. (eds), *Sources and Analogues of Chaucer's Canterbury Tales* (University of Chicago Press, 1941; repr. Humanities Press, 1958)

Burlin, R.B., *Chaucer's Fiction* (Princeton University Press, 1977)

Burnley, D.J., *Chaucer's Language and the Philosophers' Tradition* (D.S. Brewer, 1979)

—— *A Guide to Chaucer's Language* (University of Oklahoma Press, 1983)

Carruthers, M.J. and Kirk, E.D., *Acts of Interpretation: The Text in its Contexts 700-1600* (Pilgrim Books, 1982)

Cawley, A.C. (ed.), *Chaucer's Mind and Art* (Oliver and Boyd, 1969)

Cherniss, M.D., 'The Boethian Dialogue in Chaucer's *Book of the Duchess*', *JEGP* 68 (1969), pp. 655-65

—— 'Chaucer's "Anelida and Arcite", Some Conjectures', *ChR* 5 (1970), pp. 9-21

—— 'The Narrator Asleep and Awake in Chaucer's *Book of the Duchess*', *PLL* 8 (1972), pp. 115-26

—— *Boethian Apocalypse* (Pilgrim Books, 1987)

Clemen, W., *Chaucer's Early Poetry*, trans. Sym, C.A.M. (Methuen, 1963)

Cooper, H., *The Structure of the Canterbury Tales* (Duckworth, 1983)

Cowgill, B.K., 'The Parlement of Foules and the Body Politic', *JEGP* 74 (1975), pp. 315-35

Cowling, G.H., 'Chaucer's Complaintes of Mars and Venus', *RES* 2 (1926), pp. 405-10

Crow, M.M. and Olson, C.C., *The Chaucer Life-Records* (Clarendon Press, 1966)

Curry, W.C., *Chaucer and the Mediaeval Sciences* (Oxford University Press, 1926)

David, A., 'Literary Satire in the *House of Fame*', *PMLA* 75 (1960), pp. 333-9

—— 'Chaucer's Good Counsel to Scogan', *ChR* 3 (1969), pp. 265-74

—— *The Strumpet Muse. Art and Morals in Chaucer's Poetry* (Indiana University Press, 1976)

—— 'Chaucerian Comedy and Criseyde', in *Salu (1979), pp. 90-104

—— 'An ABC to the Style of the Prioress', in *Carruthers and Kirk (1982), pp. 147-57

Davis, N. *et al.*, *A Chaucer Glossary* (Clarendon Press, 1979)

Dean, N., 'Chaucer's Complaint, a Genre Descended from the

Heroides', *Comp Lit* 19 (1967), pp. 1-27

Delany, S., 'Chaucer's *Hous of Fame* and the *Ovide moralisé*', *Comp Lit* 20 (1968), pp. 254-64

—— *Chaucer's House of Fame: The Poetics of Skeptical Fideism* (University of Chicago Press, 1972)

Diamond, A., 'Chaucer's Women and Women's Chaucer' in Diamond, A. and Edwards, L.R. (eds), *The Authority of Experience: Essays in Feminist Criticism* (1977), pp. 60-83

Dodd, W.G., *Courtly Love in Chaucer and Gower* (Ginn and Co., 1913; repr. Peter Smith, 1959)

Donaldson, E.T., 'Chaucer the Pilgrim', *PMLA* 69 (1954), pp. 928-36, repr. *Schoek and Taylor, I, pp. 1-13 and in *Donaldson (1970), pp. 1-12

—— 'The Ending of Troilus', revised version: in *Donaldson (1970), pp. 84-101, repr. *Barney, pp. 115-30

—— *Speaking of Chaucer* (The Athlone Press, University of London, 1970)

—— 'The Manuscripts of Chaucer's Works and their Use', in *Brewer (1974), pp. 85-108

Donovan, M.J., 'The *Moralite* of the Nun's Priest's Sermon', *JEGP* 52 (1953), pp. 498-508

Eckhardt, C.D., 'The Medieval *Prosimetrum* Genre (from Boethius to Boece)', *Genre* 16 (1983), pp. 21-38

—— 'The Art of Translation in *The Romaunt of the Rose*', *SAC* 6 (1984), pp. 41-63

Elbow, P., *Oppositions in Chaucer* (Wesleyan University Press, 1975)

Elliott, R., *Chaucer's English* (Andre Deutsch, 1974)

Emerson, O.F., 'The Suitors in Chaucer's *Parlement of Foules*', *MP* 8 (1910), pp. 45-62

Everett, D., 'Chaucer's Good Ear', *RES* 23 (1947), pp. 201-8

Ferster, J., *Chaucer on Interpretation* (Cambridge University Press, 1985)

Fichte, J.O., *Chaucer's Art Poetical* (Gunter Narr Verlag, 1980)

Fisher, J.H., *The Complete Poetry and Prose of Geoffrey Chaucer* (Holt Rinehart and Winston, 1977)

Frank Jr., R.W., 'The Legend of *The Legend of Good Women*', *ChR* 1 (1966), pp. 110-33

—— *Chaucer and The Legend of Good Women* (Harvard University Press, 1972)

—— '*The Legend of Good Women*, Some Implications', in *Robbins (1975), pp. 63-76

French, W.H., 'The Meaning of Chaucer's *Envoy to Scogan*', *PMLA* 48 (1933), pp. 289-92

—— 'The Man in Black's Lyric', *JEGP* 61 (1957), pp. 231-41

Fry, D.K., 'The Ending of the *House of Fame*' in *Robbins (1975), pp. 27-40

Fyler, J.M., *Chaucer and Ovid* (Yale University Press, 1979)

Garrett, R.M., '"Cleopatra the martyr" and her sisters', *JEGP* 22 (1923), pp. 64-74

Gaylord, A.T., '*Sentence* and *Solaas* in Fragment VII of the *Canterbury Tales*: Harry Bailey as Horseback Editor', *PMLA* 82 (1967), pp. 226-35

—— 'Scanning the Prosodists: An essay in metacriticism', *ChR* 11 (1976), pp. 22-82

—— 'Lesson of the *Troilus*: Chastisement and Correction', in *Salu (1979), pp. 23-42

Goddard, H.C., 'Chaucer's *Legend of Good Women*', *JEGP* 7 (1907), pp. 87-129 and *JEGP* 8 (1909), pp. 47-111

Gordon, I.L., *The Double Sorrow of Troilus* (Clarendon Press, 1970)

Grennen, J.E., 'Chaucer and Chalcidius: The Platonic Origins of *The Hous of Fame*', *Viator* 15 (1984), pp. 237-62

Hansen, E.T., 'Irony and the Anti-feminist Narrator in Chaucer's *Legend of Good Women*', *JEGP* 82 (1983), pp. 11-31

Harvey, S.W., 'Chaucer's Debt to Sacrobosco', *JEGP* 34 (1935), pp. 34-8

Haveley, N.R., *Chaucer's Boccaccio* (D.S. Brewer; Rowman and Littlefield, 1980)

Hieatt, C.B., *The Realism of Dream Visions* (Mouton and Co., 1967)

Hoffman, R.L., *Ovid and the Canterbury Tales* (Oxford University Press, 1966)

Hotson, J.L., 'Colfox *vs.* Chauntecleer', *PMLA* 39 (1924), pp. 762-81, repr. *Wagenknecht, pp. 98-116

Howard, D.R., 'Chaucer the Man', *PMLA* 80 (1965), pp. 337-43

—— *The Idea of the Canterbury Tales* (University of California Press, 1976)

—— *Writers and Pilgrims* (University of California Press, 1980)

—— *Chaucer and the Medieval World* (Weidenfeld and Nicholson, 1987)

Huppé, B.F., *A Reading of the Canterbury Tales* (State University of New York, 1964)

—— and Robertson Jr., D.W., *Fruyt and Chaf* (Princeton University Press, 1963)

Jefferson, B.L., *Chaucer and the Consolation of Philosophy of Boethius* (1917; repr. Princeton University Press, 1968)

Jones, T., *Chaucer's Knight* (Weidenfeld and Nicholson, 1980)

Jordan, R.M., *Chaucer and the Shape of Creation* (Harvard University Press, 1967)
—— 'Chaucerian Romance?', *Yale French Studies* 51 (1974), pp. 223-34
—— 'The Compositional Structure of *The Book of the Duchess*', *ChR* 9 (1974), pp. 99-117
—— 'The Question of Genre: Five Chaucerian Romances', in *Robbins (1975), pp. 77-103
—— *Chaucer's Poetics and the Modern Reader* (University of California Press, 1987)
Kaminsky, A., *Chaucer's Troilus and Criseyde and the Critics* (Ohio University Press, 1980)
Kane, G., *The Autobiographical Fallacy in Chaucer and Langland Studies* (H.K. Lewis and Co. Ltd.; University College London, 1965)
Kaske, R.E., 'Clericus Adam and Chaucer's Adam Scriveyn' in *Vasta and Thundy (1979), pp. 114-18
Kean, P.M., *Chaucer and the Making of English Poetry*, 2 vols (Routledge and Kegan Paul, 1972)
Kerkhof, J., *Studies in the Language of Geoffrey Chaucer* (2nd ed., E.J. Brill; Leiden University Press, 1982)
Kiser, L.J., *Telling Classical Tales* (Cornell University Press, 1983)
Kittredge, G.L., 'Chaucer's Discussion of Marriage', *MP* 9 (1912), pp. 435-67, repr. *Schoek and Taylor, I, pp. 130-59
—— *Chaucer and His Poetry* (1915; repr. Harvard University Press, 1970)
Knight, S., *Ryming Craftily* (Angus and Robertson, 1973)
Koch, J., 'The Date and Personages of the "Parlement of Foules"', in *Essays on Chaucer, his Words and Works*, Chaucer Society, 2nd series, 18.iv (1878), pp. 400-9
Kokeritz, H., *A Guide to Chaucer's Pronunciation* (1954; repr. Toronto University Press, 1978)
Kolve, V.A., *Chaucer and the Imagery of Narrative* (Edward Arnold, 1984)
Koonce, B.G., *Chaucer and the Tradition of Fame* (Princeton University Press, 1966)
Krapp, G.P., *The Rise of English Literary Prose* (Oxford University Press, 1915)
Kreuzer, J.R., 'The Dreamer in the "Book of the Duchess"', *PMLA* 66 (1951), pp. 543-7
Laird, E.S., 'Astrology and Irony in Chaucer's *Complaint of Mars*', *ChR* 6 (1972), pp. 229-31
Lawler, T., *The One and the Many in the Canterbury Tales* (Archon, 1980)

Lawlor, J., 'The Pattern of Consolation in *The Book of the Duchess*', *Speculum* 31 (1956), pp. 626-48, repr. *Schoek and Taylor, II, pp. 232-60

Lawton, D., *Chaucer's Narrators* (D.S. Brewer, 1983)

Leicester Jr., H.M., 'The Harmony of Chaucer's *Parlement*: A Dissonant Voice', *ChR* 9 (1974), pp. 15-34

—— 'The Art of Impersonation: A General Prologue to the *Canterbury Tales*' *PMLA* 95 (1980), pp. 213-24

Lenaghan, R.T., 'Chaucer's *Envoy to Scogan*, The Uses of Literary Conventions', *ChR* 10 (1975), pp. 46-61

Lewis, C.S., 'What Chaucer Really Did to "Il Filostrato" ', *Essays and Studies by Members of the English Association* 17 (1932), pp. 56-75, repr. *Schoek and Taylor, II, pp. 16-31

—— *The Allegory of Love* (Oxford University Press, 1936)

Lipson, C., '"I n'am but a lewd compilator", Chaucer's "Treatise on the Astrolabe" as Translation', *NM* 84 (1983), pp. 192-200

Lowes, J.L., 'Is Chaucer's *Legend of Good Women* a Travesty?', *JEGP* 8 (1909), pp. 513-69

Lumiansky, R.M., 'Chaucer's *Parlement of Foules*: A Philosophical Interpretation', *RES* 24 (1948), pp. 81-9

—— *Of Sondry Folk: The Dramatic Principle in the Canterbury Tales* (University of Texas Press, 1955)

Machan, T.W., *Techniques of Translation: Chaucer's Boece* (Pilgrim Books, 1985)

Manly, J.M., 'Chaucer and the Rhetoricians', *PBA* 12 (1926), pp. 95-113, repr. *Schoek and Taylor, I, pp. 268-90

—— *Some New Light on Chaucer* (G. Bell and Sons Ltd, 1926)

—— and Rickert, E. (eds), *The Text of the 'Canterbury Tales' Studied on the Basis of All Known Manuscripts*, 8 vols (University of Chicago Press, 1940)

Mann, J., *Chaucer and Medieval Estates Satire* (Cambridge University Press, 1973)

Manning, Stephen, 'That Dreamer Once More', *PMLA* 71 (1956), pp. 540-1

Manzalaoui, M., 'Chaucer and Science', in *Brewer (1974), pp. 224-61

McAlpine, M.E., *The Genre of Troilus and Criseyde* (Cornell University Press, 1978)

McCall, J.P., 'The Harmony of Chaucer's *Parliament*', *ChR* 5 (1970), pp. 22-31

—— *Chaucer Among the Gods* (Pennsylvania State University Press, 1979)

Meech, S.B., *Design in Chaucer's Troilus* (Syracuse University Press, 1959; repr. Greenwood Press, 1969)

Miller, R.P., 'Chaucer's Pardoner, the Scriptural Eunuch and the *Pardoner's Tale*', *Speculum* 30 (1955), pp. 180-99
— (ed.), *Chaucer, Sources and Backgrounds* (Oxford University Press, 1977)
Minnis, A., *Chaucer and Pagan Antiquity* (Boydell and Brewer, 1982)
— 'From Medieval to Renaissance? Chaucer's Position on Past Gentility', *PBA* 72 (1986), pp. 205-46
Mizener, A., 'Character and Action in the Case of Criseyde', *PMLA* 54 (1939), pp. 65-81, repr. *Barney, pp. 55-74
Moore, S., 'A Further Note on the Suitors in the *Parlement of Foules*', *MLN* 26 (1911), pp. 8-12
Morse, R., 'Understanding the Man in Black', *ChR* 15 (1981), pp. 204-8
Murphy, J.M., 'A New Look at Chaucer and the Rhetoricians', *RES* ns 15 (1964), pp. 1-20
Murtaugh, D.M., 'Women and Geoffrey Chaucer', *ELH* 38 (1971), pp. 473-92
Muscatine, C., *Chaucer and the French Tradition* (University of California Press, 1957)
Nolan Jr., C.J., 'Structural Sophistication in "The Complaint Unto Pity"', *ChR* 13 (1979), pp. 363-72
North, J.D., *Chaucer's Universe* (Clarendon Press, 1988)
Norton-Smith, J., 'Chaucer's Etas Prima', *MAe* 32 (1963), pp. 117-24
— 'Chaucer's Epistolary Style', in Fowler, R. (ed.), *Essays on Style and Language* (Routledge and Kegan Paul, 1966), pp. 157-65
— *Geoffrey Chaucer* (Routledge and Kegan Paul, 1974), pp. 16-34
— 'Chaucer's *Anelida and Arcite*' in Heyworth, P.L. (ed.), *Medieval Studies for J.A.W. Bennett* (1981), pp. 81- 99
Olson, P.A., 'The *Parlement of Foules*: Aristotle's Politics and the Foundations of Human Society', *SAC* 2 (1980), pp. 52-69
— *The Canterbury Tales and the Good Society* (Princeton University Press, 1986)
Owen, C.A., 'The Role of the Narrator in the "Parliament of Fowls"', *CE* 14 (1953), pp. 264-9
— 'The Significance of Chaucer's Revisions of *Troilus and Criseyde*', *MP* 55 (1957), pp. 1-5, repr. *Schoek and Taylor, II, pp. 160-6
— 'The Transformations of a Frame Story: The Dynamics of Fiction' in *Robbins (1975), pp. 125-46
— *Pilgrimage and Storytelling in the Canterbury Tales* (University

—— 'Geoffroi Chaucier, Poete Français, Father of English Poetry',
   ChR 13 (1978), pp. 93-115
—— 'The Lyrics', in *Rowland (1979), pp. 313-31
Robertson Jr., D.W., 'Chaucerian Tragedy', *ELH* 19 (1952), pp.
   1-37, repr. *Schoek and Taylor, pp. 86-121
—— *A Preface to Chaucer: Studies in Medieval Perspective*
   (Princeton University Press, 1962)
—— 'Chaucer's Franklin and his Tale' in *Essays in Medieval Culture*
   (1980), pp. 273-90
Robinson, F.N., *The Works of Geoffrey Chaucer* (Houghton
   Mifflin, 2nd ed. 1957)
Robinson, I., *Chaucer's Prosody* (Cambridge University Press,
   1971)
—— *Chaucer and the English Tradition* (Cambridge University
   Press, 1972)
Root, R.K., *The Textual Tradition of Chaucer's Troilus*, Chaucer
   Society, first series, 99 (1916)
—— *The Book of Troilus and Criseyde. Edited from all the known
   MSS* (Princeton University Press, 1926)
Roscow, G., *Syntax and Style in Chaucer's Poetry* (D.S. Brewer;
   Rowman and Littlefield, 1981)
Rowe, D.W., *O Love, O Charite! Contraries Harmonised in
   Chaucer's Troilus* (Southern Illinois University Press; Feffer and
   Simons, 1976)
—— *Through Nature to Eternity* (University of Nebraska Press,
   1988)
Rowland, B. (ed.), *Companion to Chaucer Studies*, revised edition
   (Oxford University Press, 1979)
—— 'The Art of Memory and the Art of Poetry in the *House of Fame*',
   RUO 51 (1981), pp. 162-71
Ruggiers, P.G., 'The Unity of Chaucer's *House of Fame*', *SP* 50
   (1953), 16-29
—— *The Art of the Canterbury Tales* (University of Wisconsin
   Press, 1965)
Salter, E., 'Chaucer's "The Knight's Tale" and "The Clerk's Tale"',
   Studies in English Literature 5 (1962)
—— 'Troilus and Criseyde: A Reconsideration' in Lawlor, J.J. (ed.),
   Patterns of Love and Courtesy (Edward Arnold, 1966), pp.
   89-106
—— '*Troilus and Criseyde*: Poet and Narrator' in *Carruthers and
   Kirk (1982), pp. 281-91
—— 'Chaucer and Boccaccio: *The Knight's Tale*', in
   Fourteenth-Century English Poetry (Clarendon Press, 1983),
   pp. 141-81

Calu, M. (ed.), *Cooayo on Troiluo and Criooydo, Chauoor* Studioo 3 (1979)

Sandved, A.O., *Introduction to Chaucerian English* (D.S. Brewer, 1985)

Schlauch, M., 'Chaucer's Prose Rhythms', *PMLA* 65 (1950), pp. 568-89

—— 'The Art of Chaucer's prose' in *Brewer (1966), pp. 140-63

Schless, H., *Chaucer and Dante: a revaluation* (Pilgrim Books, 1984)

Schmidt, A.V.C., 'Chaucer and the Golden Age' in *Essays in Criticism* 26 (1976), pp. 99-115

Schoek, R.J. and Taylor, J. (eds), *Chaucer Criticism*, 2 vols (University of Notre Dame Press, 1961)

Shanley, J.L., 'The *Troilus* and Christian Love', *ELH* (1939), pp. 271-81, repr. Schoek and Taylor, II, pp. 136-46

Shoaf, R.A., '"Mutatio Amoris": "Penitentia" and the Form of *The Book of the Duchess*', *Genre* 14 (1981), pp. 163-89

Skeat, W.W. (ed.), *The Complete Works of Geoffrey Chaucer: Edited from Numerous Manuscripts*, 7 vols (Clarendon Press, 1899-1900)

Sklute, L.M., 'The Inconclusive Form of the *Parliament of Fowls*', *ChR* 16 (1981), pp. 119-28

—— *Virtue of Necessity* (Ohio State University Press, 1984)

Sledd, J., 'The *Clerk's Tale*: The Monsters and the Critics', *MP* 51 (1953), pp. 73-82, repr. *Wagenknecht, pp. 226-39 and *Schoek and Taylor, I, pp. 160-74

Southworth, J.G., 'Chaucer's Prosody: A Plea for a Reliable Text', *CE* 26 (1964), pp. 173-9, revised in *Cawley, pp. 86-96

Spearing, A.C., *Criticism and Medieval Poetry* (Edward Arnold, 1972)

—— *Medieval Dream Poetry* (Cambridge University Press, 1976)

Spurgeon, C., *Five Hundred Years of Chaucer Criticism and Allusion, 1357-1900*, 3 vols (1908-17; repr. Cambridge University Press, 1925; Russell and Russell, 1960)

Steadman, J.M., *Disembodied Laughter: Troilus and the Apotheosis Tradition* (University of California Press, 1972)

Stevenson, K., 'The Endings of Chaucer's *House of Fame*', *English Studies* 59 (1978), pp. 10-26

Stillwell, G., 'Unity and Comedy in Chaucer's *Parlement of Foules*', *JEGP* 49 (1950), pp. 470-95

Sutherland, R. (ed.), *The Romaunt of the Rose and Le Roman de la Rose* (Basil Blackwell, 1967)

Sypherd, W.O., *Studies in the Hous of Fame* (K. Paul, Trench, Trübner and Co., 1907)

—— 'The Completeness of Chaucer's *Hous of Fame*', *MLN* 30 (1915), pp. 65-8

Tatlock, J.S.P., *The Mind and Art of Chaucer* (Syracuse University Press, 1950; repr. Gordian Press, 1966)

—— and Kennedy, A.G., *A Concordance to the Complete Works of Geoffrey Chaucer and to the Romaunt of the Rose* (Carnagie Institute of Washington Publications,1927; repr. Peter Smith, 1963)

Tisdale, C.P.R., '*The House of Fame*, Virgilian Reason and Boethian Wisdom', *Comp Lit* 25 (1973), pp. 247-61

Traversi, D., *Chaucer: The Earlier Poetry* (Associated University Presses, 1987)

Vasta, E., 'To Rosemounde: Chaucer's "Gentil" Dramatic Monologue', in *Vasta and Thundy (1979), pp. 97-113

—— and Thundy, Z.P. (eds), *Chaucerian Problems and Perspectives* (University of Notre Dame Press, 1979)

Wagenknecht, E., *Chaucer: Modern Essays in Criticism* (Oxford University Press, 1959)

Wallace, D., *Chaucer and the Early Writings of Boccaccio* (Boydell and Brewer, 1985)

—— 'Chaucer's Continental Inheritance: The early poems and Troilus and Criseyde' (1986) in *Boitani and Mann, pp. 19-38

Weiss, A., 'Chaucer's Early Translations from French: The Art of Creative Transformation', in Cummins, P.W., Conner, P.W. and Connell, C.W. (eds), *Literary and Historical Perspectives of the Middle Ages* (West Virginia University Press, 1982), pp. 174-82

Wetherbee, W., *Chaucer and the Poets* (Cornell University Press, 1984)

Wheeler, B., 'Dante, Chaucer and the Ending of *Troilus and Criseyde*', *PQ* 61 (1982), pp. 105-23

Wilcockson, C., '"Thou" and "Ye" in Chaucer's *Clerk's Tale*', *The Use of English* 31 no. 3 (1980), pp. 37-43

Wilhelm, J.J., 'The Narrator and his Narrative in Chaucer's *Parlement*', *ChR* 1 (1967), pp. 201-6

Williams, G., *A New View of Chaucer* (Duke University Press, 1965)

Wimsatt, J.I., *Chaucer and the French Love Poets* (University of North Carolina Press, 1968)

—— '*Anelida and Arcite*: A Narrative of Complaint and Comfort', *ChR* 5 (1970), pp. 1-8

—— 'Guillaume de Machaut and Chaucer's Love Lyrics', *MAe* 47 (1978), pp. 66-87

—— 'Realism in *Troilus and Criseyde* and the *Roman de la Rose*' in *Salu (1979), pp. 43-56

—— '*The Book of the Duchess*: Secular Elegy or Religious Vision?', in Hermann, J.P. and Burke Jr., J.J. (eds), *Signs and Symbols in Chaucer's Poetry* (University of Alabama Press, 1981)

—— *Chaucer and the Poems of 'Ch'* (D.S. Brewer; Rowman and Littlefield, 1982)

Windeatt, B., '"Love that oughte ben secree" in Chaucer's *Troilus*', *ChR* 14 (1979), pp. 116-31

—— 'The Text of the *Troilus*' in *Salu (1979), pp. 1-22

—— *Chaucer's Dream Poetry: Sources and Analogues* (D.S. Brewer, 1982)

—— *Troilus and Criseyde: A New Edition of 'The Book of Troilus'* (Longman, 1984)

Winny, J., *Chaucer's Dream Poems* (Chatto and Windus; Barnes and Noble, 1973)

Wise, B.A., *The Influence of Statius on Chaucer* (1911; repr. Phaeton Press, 1967)

Wood, C., *Chaucer and the Country of the Stars* (Princeton University Press, 1970)

—— *The Elements of Chaucer's Troilus* (Duke University Press, 1984)

Zacher, C.K., *Curiosity and Pilgrimage* (Johns Hopkins University Press, 1976)